TEACHER'S PET PUBLICATIONS

PUZZLE PACK
for
Tears of a Tiger

based on the book by
Sharon M. Draper

Written by
Mary B. Collins

© 2009 Teacher's Pet Publications
All Rights Reserved

The materials in this packet are copyrighted
by Teacher's Pet Publications, Inc.

These pages may be duplicated by the purchaser
for use in the purchaser's own classroom.

Copying any of these materials and distributing them
for any other purpose is a violation of the copyright laws.

© 2009 Teacher's Pet Publications, Inc.
www.tpet.com

INTRODUCTION
If you already own the LitPlan for this title, this Puzzle Pack will refresh your Unit Resource Materials and Vocabulary Resource Materials sections plus give you additional materials you can substitute into the tests. If you do not already have a complete LitPlan, these pages will give you some supplemental materials to use with your own plan. There are two main groups of materials: one set for unit words (such as characters' names, symbols, places, etc.) and one set for vocabulary words associated with the book.

WORD LIST
There is a word list for both the unit words and the vocabulary words. These lists show you which words are being used in the materials and the clues or definitions being used for those words. You may want to give students a word list with clues/definitions to help them, or you may want students to only have a word list (without clues/definitions) if you want them to work a little harder. Both are available for duplication. The word lists can also be your "calling key" for the bingo games.

FILL IN THE BLANK AND MATCHING
There are 4 each of the fill in the blank and matching worksheets for both the unit and vocabulary words. These pages can be used either as extra worksheets for students or as objective parts of a unit test. They can be done individually if students need extra help or as a whole class activity to review the material covered.

MAGIC SQUARES
The magic squares not only reinforce the material covered but also work on reasoning and math skills. Many teachers have told us that their students really enjoy doing these!

WORD SEARCH PUZZLES
The word search words go in all directions, as indicated on your answer keys. Two of the word search puzzles have the clues listed rather than the words. This makes the puzzle a little more difficult, but it reinforces the material better. Two word search puzzles have words only for students who find the clue puzzles too difficult.

CROSSWORD PUZZLES
Both unit and vocabulary word sections have 4 crossword puzzles.

BINGO CARDS
There are 32 individual bingo cards for the unit words and 32 individual bingo cards for the vocabulary words. You can use your word list as a "call list," calling the words at random and marking them off of your list as you go, or you could use the flash cards by cutting them apart and drawing the words at random from a hat (or box or whatever). To make a better review, you might ask for the definition and spelling of each word as you call it out–or you could call out the definitions and have students tell you the words they need to look for on the puzzle.

JUGGLE LETTERS
The vocabulary juggle letter game is intended to help students learn the spellings of the words. One sheet has the definitions listed on it as an extra help for students who need it or to reinforce the definitions if you choose to do so.

FLASH CARDS
We've included a set of vocabulary flash cards you can duplicate, cut, and fold for your students. Some teachers make a few sets for general use by the class; others make a set for each student. Some teachers duplicate them for each student and have the students cut & fold their own. You can cut out just the words and put them in a hat, have each student pick out one word and write the definition and a sentence for that word. Students then swap words and papers, with the next student adding a sentence of his own under the last one. You can have students swap as many times as you like. Each time the student will read the sentences written prior to his own and then add a sentence. You can cut out the words and definitions separately and play "I Have; Who Has?" Each student in the room draws a word and definition. The first student says, "I have (the name of the word). Who has the definition?" The student with the definition reads it then says, "I have (the name of the vocabulary word she has). Who has the definition?" The round continues until all words and definitions have been given.

Tears Of A Tiger Word List

No.	Word	Clue/Definition
1.	ABUSE	Gerald is a victim of this.
2.	ALCOHOL	The cause of the car accident
3.	ANDREW	What Andy's dad always calls his son
4.	BANDAIDS	Gerald would get rid of peanut butter, these, and $5 bills.
5.	BASKETBALL	Andy's father did not attend any of these games.
6.	BJ	The only one not drinking the night of the accident
7.	BLACK	One teacher thinks all ___ kids are tough.
8.	CAPTAIN	Andy gets this position on the team after Rob's death.
9.	CEILING	Monty wonders why there is blood on this.
10.	COLD	Andy is worried that Rob will be ___ underground.
11.	COLLEGE	Andy's father dreams of his son going to ___.
12.	COUNSELOR	BJ and Tyrone go to see this person in hopes of helping Andy.
13.	COWARD	Andy's friends think he is a ___ for killing himself.
14.	DIE	Rhonda's most frightening moment: realizing that kids could ___
15.	DRAPER	Author
16.	DREAM	Rob haunts Andy in this.
17.	DROWNED	Andy tells his mother about a time when he was younger and almost ___.
18.	FAILURE	No son of mine is going to be a ___!
19.	FORGIVENESS	Andy asks Rob's parents for this.
20.	FRIENDS	Keisha says life without them would be boring and meaningless.
21.	GERALD	Invited but decides not to go out with the boys after the game
22.	GRAVE	Monty visited Andy there.
23.	HAZELWOOD	Name of the high school: ___ High
24.	HOMICIDE	Andy is charged with DWI and vehicular ___.
25.	JEFFERSON	Andy's last name
26.	KEISHA	Andy thinks she loves him.
27.	LAW	Andy may want to major in this.
28.	LETTER	Andy sends this to Rob's parents at his psychologist's request.
29.	MACBETH	Story Andy's class is reading when he runs out of the classroom
30.	MALL	Keisha is bored with Andy's depression & her mom picks her up there.
31.	MONTY	Andy's little brother
32.	MOVIES	Keisha is too busy to go there with Andy.
33.	NOBODY	___'s home. ___ cares....I wish I could sleep forever.
34.	NOTHING	What Andy says he sees in his future
35.	PAIN	So you're out of it and we have to stay here, feeling your ___ as well as our own.
36.	POEM	Even though Andy writes this, he doesn't turn it in for a grade.
37.	PRAY	BJ does this to help cope with the accident.
38.	PSYCHOLOGIST	Carrothers
39.	RACE	Topic of discussion after reading the snow poem
40.	RHONDA	Keisha's best friend
41.	RIPLEY	Coach who tried to help Andy
42.	ROB	Trapped in the car and burned to death
43.	ROCK	What Rob's mother would always tell Andy he got for Christmas
44.	SCOUTS	They were looking for Andy, but he wasn't at school.
45.	SHOTGUN	Andy uses this to kill himself.
46.	TALENT	Keisha and Andy break up at the ___ show.
47.	TEACHER	Andy's father brushes off her concerns.
48.	THREE	Number of people Andy tries to contact before he kills himself
49.	TIGER	Monty puts tears on this animal.

Tears Of A Tiger Word List Continued

No.	Word	Clue/Definition
50.	TYRONE	Helped Andy out of the car
51.	US	I knew better. We all did. We just never figured it would happen to __.
52.	WALL	The car hits this.
53.	WASHINGTON	Rob's last name
54.	WINTERS	One Thousand Nine Hundred Sixty-Eight ___

Tears Of A Tiger Fill In The Blanks 1

_____ 1. Andy's father brushes off her concerns.

_____ 2. Helped Andy out of the car

_____ 3. One teacher thinks all ___ kids are tough.

_____ 4. Rob's last name

_____ 5. Keisha is bored with Andy's depression & her mom picks her up there.

_____ 6. Number of people Andy tries to contact before he kills himself

_____ 7. Trapped in the car and burned to death

_____ 8. One Thousand Nine Hundred Sixty-Eight ___

_____ 9. Carrothers

_____ 10. ___'s home. ___ cares....I wish I could sleep forever.

_____ 11. Story Andy's class is reading when he runs out of the classroom

_____ 12. Andy may want to major in this.

_____ 13. Coach who tried to help Andy

_____ 14. Andy asks Rob's parents for this.

_____ 15. Rhonda's most frightening moment: realizing that kids could ___

_____ 16. So you're out of it and we have to stay here, feeling your ___ as well as our own.

_____ 17. What Andy says he sees in his future

_____ 18. Gerald is a victim of this.

_____ 19. Keisha is too busy to go there with Andy.

_____ 20. Andy uses this to kill himself.

Tears Of A Tiger Fill In The Blanks 1 Answer Key

TEACHER	1. Andy's father brushes off her concerns.
TYRONE	2. Helped Andy out of the car
BLACK	3. One teacher thinks all ___ kids are tough.
WASHINGTON	4. Rob's last name
MALL	5. Keisha is bored with Andy's depression & her mom picks her up there.
THREE	6. Number of people Andy tries to contact before he kills himself
ROB	7. Trapped in the car and burned to death
WINTERS	8. One Thousand Nine Hundred Sixty-Eight ___
PSYCHOLOGIST	9. Carrothers
NOBODY	10. ___'s home. ___ cares....I wish I could sleep forever.
MACBETH	11. Story Andy's class is reading when he runs out of the classroom
LAW	12. Andy may want to major in this.
RIPLEY	13. Coach who tried to help Andy
FORGIVENESS	14. Andy asks Rob's parents for this.
DIE	15. Rhonda's most frightening moment: realizing that kids could ___
PAIN	16. So you're out of it and we have to stay here, feeling your ___ as well as our own.
NOTHING	17. What Andy says he sees in his future
ABUSE	18. Gerald is a victim of this.
MOVIES	19. Keisha is too busy to go there with Andy.
SHOTGUN	20. Andy uses this to kill himself.

Tears Of A Tiger Fill In The Blanks 2

_____   1. Rob haunts Andy in this.
_____   2. I knew better. We all did. We just never figured it would happen to __.
_____   3. The only one not drinking the night of the accident
_____   4. Author
_____   5. What Rob's mother would always tell Andy he got for Christmas
_____   6. Keisha is too busy to go there with Andy.
_____   7. Andy is charged with DWI and vehicular ___.
_____   8. One Thousand Nine Hundred Sixty-Eight ___
_____   9. BJ and Tyrone go to see this person in hopes of helping Andy.
_____   10. Andy's father dreams of his son going to ___.
_____   11. Andy asks Rob's parents for this.
_____   12. Keisha says life without them would be boring and meaningless.
_____   13. Keisha is bored with Andy's depression & her mom picks her up there.
_____   14. The cause of the car accident
_____   15. Andy is worried that Rob will be ___ underground.
_____   16. Andy uses this to kill himself.
_____   17. Monty wonders why there is blood on this.
_____   18. Rob's last name
_____   19. Gerald is a victim of this.
_____   20. So you're out of it and we have to stay here, feeling your ___ as well as our own.

Tears Of A Tiger Fill In The Blanks 2 Answer Key

DREAM	1. Rob haunts Andy in this.
US	2. I knew better. We all did. We just never figured it would happen to __.
BJ	3. The only one not drinking the night of the accident
DRAPER	4. Author
ROCK	5. What Rob's mother would always tell Andy he got for Christmas
MOVIES	6. Keisha is too busy to go there with Andy.
HOMICIDE	7. Andy is charged with DWI and vehicular ___.
WINTERS	8. One Thousand Nine Hundred Sixty-Eight ___
COUNSELOR	9. BJ and Tyrone go to see this person in hopes of helping Andy.
COLLEGE	10. Andy's father dreams of his son going to ___.
FORGIVENESS	11. Andy asks Rob's parents for this.
FRIENDS	12. Keisha says life without them would be boring and meaningless.
MALL	13. Keisha is bored with Andy's depression & her mom picks her up there.
ALCOHOL	14. The cause of the car accident
COLD	15. Andy is worried that Rob will be ___ underground.
SHOTGUN	16. Andy uses this to kill himself.
CEILING	17. Monty wonders why there is blood on this.
WASHINGTON	18. Rob's last name
ABUSE	19. Gerald is a victim of this.
PAIN	20. So you're out of it and we have to stay here, feeling your ___ as well as our own.

Tears Of A Tiger Fill In The Blanks 3

_____

1. Andy tells his mother about a time when he was younger and almost ___.
2. Andy asks Rob's parents for this.
3. Andy's friends think he is a ___ for killing himself.
4. Rhonda's most frightening moment: realizing that kids could ___
5. Andy's last name
6. Carrothers
7. Andy's little brother
8. Monty visited Andy there.
9. BJ and Tyrone go to see this person in hopes of helping Andy.
10. Topic of discussion after reading the snow poem
11. Coach who tried to help Andy
12. Number of people Andy tries to contact before he kills himself
13. What Andy says he sees in his future
14. Invited but decides not to go out with the boys after the game
15. The cause of the car accident
16. Keisha is bored with Andy's depression & her mom picks her up there.
17. Author
18. Andy is worried that Rob will be ___ underground.
19. One teacher thinks all ___ kids are tough.
20. Gerald would get rid of peanut butter, these, and $5 bills.

Tears Of A Tiger Fill In The Blanks 3 Answer Key

DROWNED	1. Andy tells his mother about a time when he was younger and almost ___.
FORGIVENESS	2. Andy asks Rob's parents for this.
COWARD	3. Andy's friends think he is a ___ for killing himself.
DIE	4. Rhonda's most frightening moment: realizing that kids could ___
JEFFERSON	5. Andy's last name
PSYCHOLOGIST	6. Carrothers
MONTY	7. Andy's little brother
GRAVE	8. Monty visited Andy there.
COUNSELOR	9. BJ and Tyrone go to see this person in hopes of helping Andy.
RACE	10. Topic of discussion after reading the snow poem
RIPLEY	11. Coach who tried to help Andy
THREE	12. Number of people Andy tries to contact before he kills himself
NOTHING	13. What Andy says he sees in his future
GERALD	14. Invited but decides not to go out with the boys after the game
ALCOHOL	15. The cause of the car accident
MALL	16. Keisha is bored with Andy's depression & her mom picks her up there.
DRAPER	17. Author
COLD	18. Andy is worried that Rob will be ___ underground.
BLACK	19. One teacher thinks all ___ kids are tough.
BANDAIDS	20. Gerald would get rid of peanut butter, these, and $5 bills.

Tears Of A Tiger Fill In The Blanks 4

_____ 1. Andy's father did not attend any of these games.
_____ 2. Andy asks Rob's parents for this.
_____ 3. Andy thinks she loves him.
_____ 4. Trapped in the car and burned to death
_____ 5. Monty visited Andy there.
_____ 6. Even though Andy writes this, he doesn't turn it in for a grade.
_____ 7. Andy gets this position on the team after Rob's death.
_____ 8. One Thousand Nine Hundred Sixty-Eight ___
_____ 9. Gerald is a victim of this.
_____ 10. I knew better. We all did. We just never figured it would happen to __.
_____ 11. Invited but decides not to go out with the boys after the game
_____ 12. Name of the high school: ___ High
_____ 13. The only one not drinking the night of the accident
_____ 14. Keisha is too busy to go there with Andy.
_____ 15. Topic of discussion after reading the snow poem
_____ 16. The cause of the car accident
_____ 17. Andy is worried that Rob will be ___ underground.
_____ 18. Andy may want to major in this.
_____ 19. Andy is charged with DWI and vehicular ___.
_____ 20. Carrothers

Tears Of A Tiger Fill In The Blanks 4 Answer Key

BASKETBALL	1. Andy's father did not attend any of these games.
FORGIVENESS	2. Andy asks Rob's parents for this.
KEISHA	3. Andy thinks she loves him.
ROB	4. Trapped in the car and burned to death
GRAVE	5. Monty visited Andy there.
POEM	6. Even though Andy writes this, he doesn't turn it in for a grade.
CAPTAIN	7. Andy gets this position on the team after Rob's death.
WINTERS	8. One Thousand Nine Hundred Sixty-Eight ___
ABUSE	9. Gerald is a victim of this.
US	10. I knew better. We all did. We just never figured it would happen to ___.
GERALD	11. Invited but decides not to go out with the boys after the game
HAZELWOOD	12. Name of the high school: ___ High
BJ	13. The only one not drinking the night of the accident
MOVIES	14. Keisha is too busy to go there with Andy.
RACE	15. Topic of discussion after reading the snow poem
ALCOHOL	16. The cause of the car accident
COLD	17. Andy is worried that Rob will be ___ underground.
LAW	18. Andy may want to major in this.
HOMICIDE	19. Andy is charged with DWI and vehicular ___.
PSYCHOLOGIST	20. Carrothers

Tears Of A Tiger Matching 1

___ 1. COLLEGE   A. Carrothers
___ 2. COUNSELOR   B. Keisha says life without them would be boring and meaningless.
___ 3. ROB   C. What Andy's dad always calls his son
___ 4. COLD   D. Trapped in the car and burned to death
___ 5. MONTY   E. Monty visited Andy there.
___ 6. PAIN   F. Keisha's best friend
___ 7. ABUSE   G. Andy uses this to kill himself.
___ 8. SHOTGUN   H. BJ does this to help cope with the accident.
___ 9. PSYCHOLOGIST   I. So you're out of it and we have to stay here, feeling your ___ as well as our own.
___10. ANDREW   J. Invited but decides not to go out with the boys after the game
___11. FRIENDS   K. Andy's friends think he is a ___ for killing himself.
___12. ALCOHOL   L. BJ and Tyrone go to see this person in hopes of helping Andy.
___13. GRAVE   M. Gerald would get rid of peanut butter, these, and $5 bills.
___14. BANDAIDS   N. Andy is worried that Rob will be ___ underground.
___15. HAZELWOOD   O. Gerald is a victim of this.
___16. GERALD   P. Andy's little brother
___17. WASHINGTON   Q. The cause of the car accident
___18. COWARD   R. Andy's father dreams of his son going to ___.
___19. RHONDA   S. Name of the high school: ___ High
___20. PRAY   T. Rob's last name

Tears Of A Tiger Matching 1 Answer Key

R - 1. COLLEGE	A.	Carrothers
L - 2. COUNSELOR	B.	Keisha says life without them would be boring and meaningless.
D - 3. ROB	C.	What Andy's dad always calls his son
N - 4. COLD	D.	Trapped in the car and burned to death
P - 5. MONTY	E.	Monty visited Andy there.
I - 6. PAIN	F.	Keisha's best friend
O - 7. ABUSE	G.	Andy uses this to kill himself.
G - 8. SHOTGUN	H.	BJ does this to help cope with the accident.
A - 9. PSYCHOLOGIST	I.	So you're out of it and we have to stay here, feeling your ___ as well as our own.
C - 10. ANDREW	J.	Invited but decides not to go out with the boys after the game
B - 11. FRIENDS	K.	Andy's friends think he is a ___ for killing himself.
Q - 12. ALCOHOL	L.	BJ and Tyrone go to see this person in hopes of helping Andy.
E - 13. GRAVE	M.	Gerald would get rid of peanut butter, these, and $5 bills.
M - 14. BANDAIDS	N.	Andy is worried that Rob will be ___ underground.
S - 15. HAZELWOOD	O.	Gerald is a victim of this.
J - 16. GERALD	P.	Andy's little brother
T - 17. WASHINGTON	Q.	The cause of the car accident
K - 18. COWARD	R.	Andy's father dreams of his son going to ___.
F - 19. RHONDA	S.	Name of the high school: ___ High
H - 20. PRAY	T.	Rob's last name

Tears Of A Tiger Matching 2

___ 1. GERALD   A. BJ does this to help cope with the accident.
___ 2. BLACK   B. Coach who tried to help Andy
___ 3. RIPLEY   C. Monty visited Andy there.
___ 4. MONTY   D. Invited but decides not to go out with the boys after the game
___ 5. COUNSELOR   E. Gerald is a victim of this.
___ 6. LETTER   F. Andy's father dreams of his son going to ___.
___ 7. WALL   G. Keisha's best friend
___ 8. COLLEGE   H. What Rob's mother would always tell Andy he got for Christmas
___ 9. HAZELWOOD   I. The car hits this.
___10. ROCK   J. Andy tells his mother about a time when he was younger and almost ___.
___11. RHONDA   K. Andy's little brother
___12. MALL   L. Author
___13. PRAY   M. One teacher thinks all ___ kids are tough.
___14. BANDAIDS   N. Rhonda's most frightening moment: realizing that kids could ___
___15. ABUSE   O. Andy's father did not attend any of these games.
___16. DRAPER   P. Name of the high school: ___ High
___17. BASKETBALL   Q. Andy sends this to Rob's parents at his psychologist's request.
___18. DROWNED   R. Keisha is bored with Andy's depression & her mom picks her up there.
___19. DIE   S. BJ and Tyrone go to see this person in hopes of helping Andy.
___20. GRAVE   T. Gerald would get rid of peanut butter, these, and $5 bills.

Tears Of A Tiger Matching 2 Answer Key

D - 1. GERALD	A. BJ does this to help cope with the accident.
M - 2. BLACK	B. Coach who tried to help Andy
B - 3. RIPLEY	C. Monty visited Andy there.
K - 4. MONTY	D. Invited but decides not to go out with the boys after the game
S - 5. COUNSELOR	E. Gerald is a victim of this.
Q - 6. LETTER	F. Andy's father dreams of his son going to ___.
I - 7. WALL	G. Keisha's best friend
F - 8. COLLEGE	H. What Rob's mother would always tell Andy he got for Christmas
P - 9. HAZELWOOD	I. The car hits this.
H -10. ROCK	J. Andy tells his mother about a time when he was younger and almost ___.
G -11. RHONDA	K. Andy's little brother
R -12. MALL	L. Author
A -13. PRAY	M. One teacher thinks all ___ kids are tough.
T -14. BANDAIDS	N. Rhonda's most frightening moment: realizing that kids could ___
E -15. ABUSE	O. Andy's father did not attend any of these games.
L -16. DRAPER	P. Name of the high school: ___ High
O -17. BASKETBALL	Q. Andy sends this to Rob's parents at his psychologist's request.
J -18. DROWNED	R. Keisha is bored with Andy's depression & her mom picks her up there.
N -19. DIE	S. BJ and Tyrone go to see this person in hopes of helping Andy.
C -20. GRAVE	T. Gerald would get rid of peanut butter, these, and $5 bills.

Tears Of A Tiger Matching 3

___ 1. POEM
___ 2. DROWNED
___ 3. RIPLEY
___ 4. PSYCHOLOGIST
___ 5. DIE
___ 6. ROCK
___ 7. LETTER
___ 8. CAPTAIN
___ 9. COUNSELOR
___ 10. DRAPER
___ 11. BLACK
___ 12. TYRONE
___ 13. NOTHING
___ 14. FAILURE
___ 15. BANDAIDS
___ 16. CEILING
___ 17. WASHINGTON
___ 18. GERALD
___ 19. RACE
___ 20. HOMICIDE

A. Rob's last name
B. Andy sends this to Rob's parents at his psychologist's request.
C. Topic of discussion after reading the snow poem
D. What Rob's mother would always tell Andy he got for Christmas
E. Andy is charged with DWI and vehicular ___.
F. Andy gets this position on the team after Rob's death.
G. BJ and Tyrone go to see this person in hopes of helping Andy.
H. One teacher thinks all ___ kids are tough.
I. Andy tells his mother about a time when he was younger and almost ___.
J. Helped Andy out of the car
K. Rhonda's most frightening moment: realizing that kids could ___
L. Coach who tried to help Andy
M. Carrothers
N. Invited but decides not to go out with the boys after the game
O. What Andy says he sees in his future
P. Gerald would get rid of peanut butter, these, and $5 bills.
Q. Even though Andy writes this, he doesn't turn it in for a grade.
R. Monty wonders why there is blood on this.
S. No son of mine is going to be a ___!
T. Author

Tears Of A Tiger Matching 3 Answer Key

Q - 1.	POEM	A. Rob's last name
I - 2.	DROWNED	B. Andy sends this to Rob's parents at his psychologist's request.
L - 3.	RIPLEY	C. Topic of discussion after reading the snow poem
M - 4.	PSYCHOLOGIST	D. What Rob's mother would always tell Andy he got for Christmas
K - 5.	DIE	E. Andy is charged with DWI and vehicular ___.
D - 6.	ROCK	F. Andy gets this position on the team after Rob's death.
B - 7.	LETTER	G. BJ and Tyrone go to see this person in hopes of helping Andy.
F - 8.	CAPTAIN	H. One teacher thinks all ___ kids are tough.
G - 9.	COUNSELOR	I. Andy tells his mother about a time when he was younger and almost ___.
T - 10.	DRAPER	J. Helped Andy out of the car
H - 11.	BLACK	K. Rhonda's most frightening moment: realizing that kids could ___.
J - 12.	TYRONE	L. Coach who tried to help Andy
O - 13.	NOTHING	M. Carrothers
S - 14.	FAILURE	N. Invited but decides not to go out with the boys after the game
P - 15.	BANDAIDS	O. What Andy says he sees in his future
R - 16.	CEILING	P. Gerald would get rid of peanut butter, these, and $5 bills.
A - 17.	WASHINGTON	Q. Even though Andy writes this, he doesn't turn it in for a grade.
N - 18.	GERALD	R. Monty wonders why there is blood on this.
C - 19.	RACE	S. No son of mine is going to be a ___!
E - 20.	HOMICIDE	T. Author

Tears Of A Tiger Matching 4

___ 1. TALENT   A. Name of the high school: ___ High
___ 2. PRAY   B. Andy's friends think he is a ___ for killing himself.
___ 3. ALCOHOL   C. Keisha and Andy break up at the ___ show.
___ 4. NOBODY   D. Gerald would get rid of peanut butter, these, and $5 bills.
___ 5. RIPLEY   E. The cause of the car accident
___ 6. WASHINGTON   F. Gerald is a victim of this.
___ 7. HAZELWOOD   G. What Andy says he sees in his future
___ 8. MACBETH   H. ___'s home. ___ cares....I wish I could sleep forever.
___ 9. BLACK   I. What Andy's dad always calls his son
___ 10. PSYCHOLOGIST J. Story Andy's class is reading when he runs out of the classroom
___ 11. CAPTAIN   K. One teacher thinks all ___ kids are tough.
___ 12. BANDAIDS   L. Author
___ 13. NOTHING   M. Monty puts tears on this animal.
___ 14. RACE   N. Andy's little brother
___ 15. DRAPER   O. BJ does this to help cope with the accident.
___ 16. MONTY   P. Rob's last name
___ 17. ABUSE   Q. Topic of discussion after reading the snow poem
___ 18. TIGER   R. Andy gets this position on the team after Rob's death.
___ 19. ANDREW   S. Coach who tried to help Andy
___ 20. COWARD   T. Carrothers

Tears Of A Tiger Matching 4 Answer Key

C - 1. TALENT	A. Name of the high school: ___ High
O - 2. PRAY	B. Andy's friends think he is a ___ for killing himself.
E - 3. ALCOHOL	C. Keisha and Andy break up at the ___ show.
H - 4. NOBODY	D. Gerald would get rid of peanut butter, these, and $5 bills.
S - 5. RIPLEY	E. The cause of the car accident
P - 6. WASHINGTON	F. Gerald is a victim of this.
A - 7. HAZELWOOD	G. What Andy says he sees in his future
J - 8. MACBETH	H. ___'s home. ___ cares....I wish I could sleep forever.
K - 9. BLACK	I. What Andy's dad always calls his son
T - 10. PSYCHOLOGIST	J. Story Andy's class is reading when he runs out of the classroom
R - 11. CAPTAIN	K. One teacher thinks all ___ kids are tough.
D - 12. BANDAIDS	L. Author
G - 13. NOTHING	M. Monty puts tears on this animal.
Q - 14. RACE	N. Andy's little brother
L - 15. DRAPER	O. BJ does this to help cope with the accident.
N - 16. MONTY	P. Rob's last name
F - 17. ABUSE	Q. Topic of discussion after reading the snow poem
M - 18. TIGER	R. Andy gets this position on the team after Rob's death.
I - 19. ANDREW	S. Coach who tried to help Andy
B - 20. COWARD	T. Carrothers

Tears Of A Tiger Magic Squares 1

Match the definition with the vocabulary word. Put your answers in the magic squares below. When your answers are correct, all columns and rows will add to the same number.

A. WALL
B. LAW
C. DROWNED
D. MACBETH
E. THREE
F. POEM
G. BASKETBALL
H. BJ
I. SCOUTS
J. RACE
K. TYRONE
L. GERALD
M. PRAY
N. US
O. CEILING
P. TEACHER

1. Monty wonders why there is blood on this.
2. Story Andy's class is reading when he runs out of the classroom
3. Topic of discussion after reading the snow poem
4. Number of people Andy tries to contact before he kills himself
5. They were looking for Andy, but he wasn't at school.
6. Even though Andy writes this, he doesn't turn it in for a grade.
7. Andy's father brushes off her concerns.
8. Andy tells his mother about a time when he was younger and almost ___.
9. The only one not drinking the night of the accident
10. Helped Andy out of the car
11. The car hits this.
12. I knew better. We all did. We just never figured it would happen to ___.
13. Andy may want to major in this.
14. BJ does this to help cope with the accident.
15. Andy's father did not attend any of these games.
16. Invited but decides not to go out with the boys after the game

A=	B=	C=	D=
E=	F=	G=	H=
I=	J=	K=	L=
M=	N=	O=	P=

Tears Of A Tiger Magic Squares 1 Answer Key

Match the definition with the vocabulary word. Put your answers in the magic squares below. When your answers are correct, all columns and rows will add to the same number.

A. WALL
B. LAW
C. DROWNED
D. MACBETH
E. THREE
F. POEM
G. BASKETBALL
H. BJ
I. SCOUTS
J. RACE
K. TYRONE
L. GERALD
M. PRAY
N. US
O. CEILING
P. TEACHER

1. Monty wonders why there is blood on this.
2. Story Andy's class is reading when he runs out of the classroom
3. Topic of discussion after reading the snow poem
4. Number of people Andy tries to contact before he kills himself
5. They were looking for Andy, but he wasn't at school.
6. Even though Andy writes this, he doesn't turn it in for a grade.
7. Andy's father brushes off her concerns.
8. Andy tells his mother about a time when he was younger and almost ___.
9. The only one not drinking the night of the accident
10. Helped Andy out of the car
11. The car hits this.
12. I knew better. We all did. We just never figured it would happen to ___.
13. Andy may want to major in this.
14. BJ does this to help cope with the accident.
15. Andy's father did not attend any of these games.
16. Invited but decides not to go out with the boys after the game

A=11	B=13	C=8	D=2
E=4	F=6	G=15	H=9
I=5	J=3	K=10	L=16
M=14	N=12	O=1	P=7

Tears Of A Tiger Magic Squares 2

Match the definition with the vocabulary word. Put your answers in the magic squares below. When your answers are correct, all columns and rows will add to the same number.

A. MONTY   E. SHOTGUN   I. PRAY   M. ALCOHOL
B. THREE   F. PSYCHOLOGIST   J. NOTHING   N. KEISHA
C. COLD   G. MACBETH   K. JEFFERSON   O. US
D. RACE   H. WINTERS   L. COWARD   P. TYRONE

1. The cause of the car accident
2. Carrothers
3. One Thousand Nine Hundred Sixty-Eight ___
4. I knew better. We all did. We just never figured it would happen to __.
5. Andy's friends think he is a ___ for killing himself.
6. Andy is worried that Rob will be ___ underground.
7. Andy's little brother
8. What Andy says he sees in his future
9. Andy's last name
10. Topic of discussion after reading the snow poem
11. Number of people Andy tries to contact before he kills himself
12. BJ does this to help cope with the accident.
13. Andy thinks she loves him.
14. Andy uses this to kill himself.
15. Story Andy's class is reading when he runs out of the classroom
16. Helped Andy out of the car

A=	B=	C=	D=
E=	F=	G=	H=
I=	J=	K=	L=
M=	N=	O=	P=

Tears Of A Tiger Magic Squares 2 Answer Key

Match the definition with the vocabulary word. Put your answers in the magic squares below. When your answers are correct, all columns and rows will add to the same number.

A. MONTY
B. THREE
C. COLD
D. RACE
E. SHOTGUN
F. PSYCHOLOGIST
G. MACBETH
H. WINTERS
I. PRAY
J. NOTHING
K. JEFFERSON
L. COWARD
M. ALCOHOL
N. KEISHA
O. US
P. TYRONE

1. The cause of the car accident
2. Carrothers
3. One Thousand Nine Hundred Sixty-Eight ___
4. I knew better. We all did. We just never figured it would happen to __.
5. Andy's friends think he is a ___ for killing himself.
6. Andy is worried that Rob will be ___ underground.
7. Andy's little brother
8. What Andy says he sees in his future
9. Andy's last name
10. Topic of discussion after reading the snow poem
11. Number of people Andy tries to contact before he kills himself
12. BJ does this to help cope with the accident.
13. Andy thinks she loves him.
14. Andy uses this to kill himself.
15. Story Andy's class is reading when he runs out of the classroom
16. Helped Andy out of the car

A=7	B=11	C=6	D=10
E=14	F=2	G=15	H=3
I=12	J=8	K=9	L=5
M=1	N=13	O=4	P=16

Tears Of A Tiger Magic Squares 3

Match the definition with the vocabulary word. Put your answers in the magic squares below. When your answers are correct, all columns and rows will add to the same number.

A. BASKETBALL E. DRAPER I. MACBETH M. NOTHING
B. ABUSE F. HOMICIDE J. NOBODY N. COWARD
C. ROCK G. ALCOHOL K. ROB O. DIE
D. FORGIVENESS H. GERALD L. FAILURE P. BANDAIDS

1. Andy's friends think he is a ___ for killing himself.
2. The cause of the car accident
3. No son of mine is going to be a ___!
4. Andy's father did not attend any of these games.
5. Trapped in the car and burned to death
6. Gerald is a victim of this.
7. What Andy says he sees in his future
8. Invited but decides not to go out with the boys after the game
9. Author
10. Gerald would get rid of peanut butter, these, and $5 bills.
11. What Rob's mother would always tell Andy he got for Christmas
12. ___'s home. ___ cares....I wish I could sleep forever.
13. Andy asks Rob's parents for this.
14. Story Andy's class is reading when he runs out of the classroom
15. Andy is charged with DWI and vehicular ___.
16. Rhonda's most frightening moment: realizing that kids could ___

A=	B=	C=	D=
E=	F=	G=	H=
I=	J=	K=	L=
M=	N=	O=	P=

Tears Of A Tiger Magic Squares 3 Answer Key

Match the definition with the vocabulary word. Put your answers in the magic squares below. When your answers are correct, all columns and rows will add to the same number.

A. BASKETBALL E. DRAPER   I. MACBETH   M. NOTHING
B. ABUSE   F. HOMICIDE   J. NOBODY   N. COWARD
C. ROCK   G. ALCOHOL   K. ROB   O. DIE
D. FORGIVENESS H. GERALD   L. FAILURE   P. BANDAIDS

1. Andy's friends think he is a ___ for killing himself.
2. The cause of the car accident
3. No son of mine is going to be a ___!
4. Andy's father did not attend any of these games.
5. Trapped in the car and burned to death
6. Gerald is a victim of this.
7. What Andy says he sees in his future
8. Invited but decides not to go out with the boys after the game
9. Author
10. Gerald would get rid of peanut butter, these, and $5 bills.
11. What Rob's mother would always tell Andy he got for Christmas
12. ___'s home. ___ cares....I wish I could sleep forever.
13. Andy asks Rob's parents for this.
14. Story Andy's class is reading when he runs out of the classroom
15. Andy is charged with DWI and vehicular ___.
16. Rhonda's most frightening moment: realizing that kids could ___

A=4	B=6	C=11	D=13
E=9	F=15	G=2	H=8
I=14	J=12	K=5	L=3
M=7	N=1	O=16	P=10

Tears Of A Tiger Magic Squares 4

Match the definition with the vocabulary word. Put your answers in the magic squares below. When your answers are correct, all columns and rows will add to the same number.

A. ABUSE   E. MACBETH   I. PAIN   M. SHOTGUN
B. BJ   F. COLLEGE   J. TALENT   N. KEISHA
C. LETTER   G. HOMICIDE   K. BLACK   O. TEACHER
D. ALCOHOL   H. COWARD   L. FORGIVENESS   P. TYRONE

1. Andy sends this to Rob's parents at his psychologist's request.
2. Keisha and Andy break up at the ___ show.
3. Andy's father dreams of his son going to ___.
4. Andy's father brushes off her concerns.
5. Helped Andy out of the car
6. Story Andy's class is reading when he runs out of the classroom
7. So you're out of it and we have to stay here, feeling your ___ as well as our own.
8. The cause of the car accident
9. Andy uses this to kill himself.
10. Andy's friends think he is a ___ for killing himself.
11. Andy asks Rob's parents for this.
12. Gerald is a victim of this.
13. The only one not drinking the night of the accident
14. One teacher thinks all ___ kids are tough.
15. Andy is charged with DWI and vehicular ___.
16. Andy thinks she loves him.

A=	B=	C=	D=
E=	F=	G=	H=
I=	J=	K=	L=
M=	N=	O=	P=

Tears Of A Tiger Magic Squares 4 Answer Key

Match the definition with the vocabulary word. Put your answers in the magic squares below. When your answers are correct, all columns and rows will add to the same number.

A. ABUSE
B. BJ
C. LETTER
D. ALCOHOL
E. MACBETH
F. COLLEGE
G. HOMICIDE
H. COWARD
I. PAIN
J. TALENT
K. BLACK
L. FORGIVENESS
M. SHOTGUN
N. KEISHA
O. TEACHER
P. TYRONE

1. Andy sends this to Rob's parents at his psychologist's request.
2. Keisha and Andy break up at the ___ show.
3. Andy's father dreams of his son going to ___.
4. Andy's father brushes off her concerns.
5. Helped Andy out of the car
6. Story Andy's class is reading when he runs out of the classroom
7. So you're out of it and we have to stay here, feeling your ___ as well as our own.
8. The cause of the car accident
9. Andy uses this to kill himself.
10. Andy's friends think he is a ___ for killing himself.
11. Andy asks Rob's parents for this.
12. Gerald is a victim of this.
13. The only one not drinking the night of the accident
14. One teacher thinks all ___ kids are tough.
15. Andy is charged with DWI and vehicular ___.
16. Andy thinks she loves him.

A=12	B=13	C=1	D=8
E=6	F=3	G=15	H=10
I=7	J=2	K=14	L=11
M=9	N=16	O=4	P=5

Tears Of A Tiger Word Search 1

```
N O B O D Y F Z R W G F B M R C R
R C P R A Y N T A L E N T K A O T
M Q E R X I X S C C R I C G L L B
N A Z V A R H S E B A A P E N D L
M Y N T H I C D I E L P S W O B B
G O P O N O J R B D N Y A T A F
T A N G U C Q U R C U P C L H S Y
C D T T R E L R O O B O H L I K Z
A O S K Y I H D C Y C E O H N E P
N W H D A L P P K R O M L O G T Y
D I O F B I U L L A W W O M M B Z
R N T J U N S K E V A R G I O A Y
E T G T S G D H D Y R M I C V L L
W E U X E F R I E N D S S I L L
D R N A L C O H O L K B T D E S G
P S H A Z E L W O O D M J E S W X
```

Andy gets this position on the team after Rob's death. (7)
Andy is charged with DWI and vehicular ___. (8)
Andy is worried that Rob will be ___ underground. (4)
Andy may want to major in this. (3)
Andy uses this to kill himself. (7)
Andy's father did not attend any of these games. (10)
Andy's friends think he is a ___ for killing himself. (6)
Andy's little brother (5)
BJ and Tyrone go to see this person in hopes of helping Andy. (9)
BJ does this to help cope with the accident. (4)
Carrothers (12)
Coach who tried to help Andy (6)
Even though Andy writes this, he doesn't turn it in for a grade. (4)
Gerald is a victim of this. (5)
I knew better. We all did. We just never figured it would happen to __. (2)
Invited but decides not to go out with the boys after the game (6)
Keisha and Andy break up at the ___ show. (6)
Keisha is bored with Andy's depression & her mom picks her up there. (4)
Keisha is too busy to go there with Andy. (6)
Keisha says life without them would be boring and meaningless. (7)

Keisha's best friend (6)
Monty visited Andy there. (5)
Monty wonders why there is blood on this. (7)
Name of the high school: ___ High (9)
No son of mine is going to be a ___! (7)
One Thousand Nine Hundred Sixty-Eight ___ (7)
One teacher thinks all ___ kids are tough. (5)
Rhonda's most frightening moment: realizing that kids could ___ (3)
Rob haunts Andy in this. (5)
Rob's last name (10)
So you're out of it and we have to stay here, feeling your ___ as well as our own. (4)
The car hits this. (4)
The cause of the car accident (7)
The only one not drinking the night of the accident (2)
They were looking for Andy, but he wasn't at school. (6)
Topic of discussion after reading the snow poem (4)
Trapped in the car and burned to death (3)
What Andy says he sees in his future (7)
What Andy's dad always calls his son (6)
What Rob's mother would always tell Andy he got for Christmas (4)
___'s home. ___ cares....I wish I could sleep forever. (6)

Tears Of A Tiger Word Search 1 Answer Key

Andy gets this position on the team after Rob's death. (7)
Andy is charged with DWI and vehicular ___. (8)
Andy is worried that Rob will be ___ underground. (4)
Andy may want to major in this. (3)
Andy uses this to kill himself. (7)
Andy's father did not attend any of these games. (10)
Andy's friends think he is a ___ for killing himself. (6)
Andy's little brother (5)
BJ and Tyrone go to see this person in hopes of helping Andy. (9)
BJ does this to help cope with the accident. (4)
Carrothers (12)
Coach who tried to help Andy (6)
Even though Andy writes this, he doesn't turn it in for a grade. (4)
Gerald is a victim of this. (5)
I knew better. We all did. We just never figured it would happen to __. (2)
Invited but decides not to go out with the boys after the game (6)
Keisha and Andy break up at the ___ show. (6)
Keisha is bored with Andy's depression & her mom picks her up there. (4)
Keisha is too busy to go there with Andy. (6)
Keisha says life without them would be boring and meaningless. (7)

Keisha's best friend (6)
Monty visited Andy there. (5)
Monty wonders why there is blood on this. (7)
Name of the high school: ___ High (9)
No son of mine is going to be a ___! (7)
One Thousand Nine Hundred Sixty-Eight ___ (7)
One teacher thinks all ___ kids are tough. (5)
Rhonda's most frightening moment: realizing that kids could ___ (3)
Rob haunts Andy in this. (5)
Rob's last name (10)
So you're out of it and we have to stay here, feeling your ___ as well as our own. (4)
The car hits this. (4)
The cause of the car accident (7)
The only one not drinking the night of the accident (2)
They were looking for Andy, but he wasn't at school. (6)
Topic of discussion after reading the snow poem (4)
Trapped in the car and burned to death (3)
What Andy says he sees in his future (7)
What Andy's dad always calls his son (6)
What Rob's mother would always tell Andy he got for Christmas (4)
___'s home. ___ cares....I wish I could sleep forever. (6)

Tears Of A Tiger Word Search 2

```
T F B R Y A L G L P Q L D R E A M
A H A A F R N L S S B O E S U B A
L Y R I N I I D X D C H B T L K V
E P J E L D R P R K C O R C T X K
N V F I E U A H L E R C U K O E N
T P E S G N R I O E W L R T M L R
M C T H H X N E D N Y A C D S X D
R Q Y O E O W Z K S D M L R D C V
F Y R T G S M O N T Y A Y O O V S
T G O G E V T I W V R M O W S F R
D Y N U L R F D C E Y W A H T H E
R D E N L G N B G I L R S I M N T
A O W M O E R M M E D K G Q L I N
P B L A C K E A Z D K E I S H A I
E O B A L O L A V I R B G Q U P W
R N R J P L H N S E I V O M R S D
```

Andy is charged with DWI and vehicular ___. (8)
Andy is worried that Rob will be ___ underground. (4)
Andy may want to major in this. (3)
Andy sends this to Rob's parents at his psychologist's request. (6)
Andy thinks she loves him. (6)
Andy uses this to kill himself. (7)
Andy's father dreams of his son going to ___. (7)
Andy's friends think he is a ___ for killing himself. (6)
Andy's little brother (5)
Author (6)
BJ does this to help cope with the accident. (4)
Coach who tried to help Andy (6)
Even though Andy writes this, he doesn't turn it in for a grade. (4)
Gerald is a victim of this. (5)
Gerald would get rid of peanut butter, these, and $5 bills. (8)
Helped Andy out of the car (6)
I knew better. We all did. We just never figured it would happen to ___. (2)
Invited but decides not to go out with the boys after the game (6)
Keisha and Andy break up at the ___ show. (6)
Keisha is bored with Andy's depression & her mom picks her up there. (4)
Keisha is too busy to go there with Andy. (6)
Keisha's best friend (6)
Monty puts tears on this animal. (5)
Monty visited Andy there. (5)
Monty wonders why there is blood on this. (7)
Name of the high school: ___ High (9)
No son of mine is going to be a ___! (7)
Number of people Andy tries to contact before he kills himself (5)
One Thousand Nine Hundred Sixty-Eight ___ (7)
One teacher thinks all ___ kids are tough. (5)
Rhonda's most frightening moment: realizing that kids could ___ (3)
Rob haunts Andy in this. (5)
So you're out of it and we have to stay here, feeling your ___ as well as our own. (4)
The car hits this. (4)
The cause of the car accident (7)
The only one not drinking the night of the accident (2)
They were looking for Andy, but he wasn't at school. (6)
Topic of discussion after reading the snow poem (4)
Trapped in the car and burned to death (3)
What Andy's dad always calls his son (6)
What Rob's mother would always tell Andy he got for Christmas (4)
___'s home. ___ cares....I wish I could sleep forever. (6)

Tears Of A Tiger Word Search 2 Answer Key

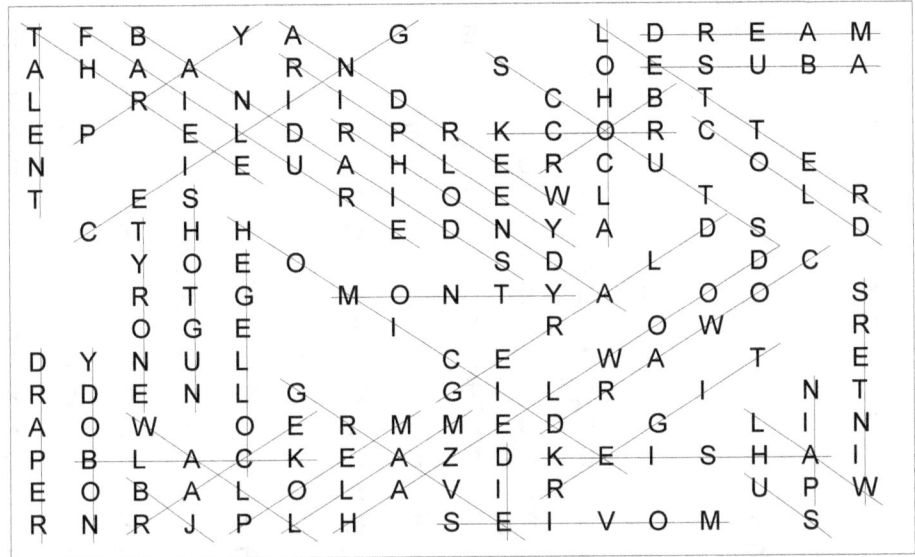

Andy is charged with DWI and vehicular ___. (8)
Andy is worried that Rob will be ___ underground. (4)
Andy may want to major in this. (3)
Andy sends this to Rob's parents at his psychologist's request. (6)
Andy thinks she loves him. (6)
Andy uses this to kill himself. (7)
Andy's father dreams of his son going to ___. (7)
Andy's friends think he is a ___ for killing himself. (6)
Andy's little brother (5)
Author (6)
BJ does this to help cope with the accident. (4)
Coach who tried to help Andy (6)
Even though Andy writes this, he doesn't turn it in for a grade. (4)
Gerald is a victim of this. (5)
Gerald would get rid of peanut butter, these, and $5 bills. (8)
Helped Andy out of the car (6)
I knew better. We all did. We just never figured it would happen to __. (2)
Invited but decides not to go out with the boys after the game (6)
Keisha and Andy break up at the ___ show. (6)
Keisha is bored with Andy's depression & her mom picks her up there. (4)
Keisha is too busy to go there with Andy. (6)
Keisha's best friend (6)

Monty puts tears on this animal. (5)
Monty visited Andy there. (5)
Monty wonders why there is blood on this. (7)
Name of the high school: ___ High (9)
No son of mine is going to be a ___! (7)
Number of people Andy tries to contact before he kills himself (5)
One Thousand Nine Hundred Sixty-Eight ___ (7)
One teacher thinks all ___ kids are tough. (5)
Rhonda's most frightening moment: realizing that kids could ___ (3)
Rob haunts Andy in this. (5)
So you're out of it and we have to stay here, feeling your ___ as well as our own. (4)
The car hits this. (4)
The cause of the car accident (7)
The only one not drinking the night of the accident (2)
They were looking for Andy, but he wasn't at school. (6)
Topic of discussion after reading the snow poem (4)
Trapped in the car and burned to death (3)
What Andy's dad always calls his son (6)
What Rob's mother would always tell Andy he got for Christmas (4)
___'s home. ___ cares....I wish I could sleep forever. (6)

Tears Of A Tiger Word Search 3

```
P N D D H B L A C K E L E G R A V E B F
S O R W G O A W B N L G I H R L B S J C
Y T E C Z R A W O A E G D S H O C U Z T
C G A M A Y Y R W L H R I W N O S G S T
H N M V P Y D L O C E U S D H K E D E
O I S R W T T O Y Q K T C E A O E R R J
L H P B J K C A L N R N O I V L T A O K
O S M A G Y R H I T D I U V S H B L W C
G A A N I E I T N N H W N O K Z A D N D
I W L D P N P E H F N R S M R F L R E K
S W L A P V L B O O O F E C R B L A D H
T N R I V A E C M R T A L E E R O C K L
P D E D T Q Y A I G H I O E T I Z E N M
C M G S V M T M C I L R V T C L Z S B
V M I P G M N D I V N U H H A T H I D H
F L T V P H O H D E G R M N N H E P N C
S C O U T S M P E N C E W L D P K R E G
S J R M D O O W L E Z A H H R F Q M I F
N O B O D Y J N O S R E F F E J L K R W
T E A C H E R K F S P D R A W O C S F D
```

ABUSE	COUNSELOR	HAZELWOOD	NOTHING	TALENT
ALCOHOL	COWARD	HOMICIDE	PAIN	TEACHER
ANDREW	DIE	JEFFERSON	POEM	THREE
BANDAIDS	DRAPER	KEISHA	PRAY	TIGER
BASKETBALL	DREAM	LAW	PSYCHOLOGIST	TYRONE
BJ	DROWNED	LETTER	RACE	US
BLACK	FAILURE	MACBETH	RHONDA	WALL
CAPTAIN	FORGIVENESS	MALL	RIPLEY	WASHINGTON
CEILING	FRIENDS	MONTY	ROB	WINTERS
COLD	GERALD	MOVIES	ROCK	
COLLEGE	GRAVE	NOBODY	SCOUTS	

Copyrighted

Tears Of A Tiger Word Search 3 Answer Key

```
P  N   D         B L A C K E L E G R A V E B
S  O   R         O A     N   G I   H   B   J
Y  T   E     C   R W     O A E S D S O C A   U
C  G   A   M A Y   R W   A L   R   I   N O   G E
H  N   M   A P T   Y D L O C K E   U S D H O K E
O  I       R B T   T O     K T   C   A O S E   D
L  H   P   B A C   C H     I N I   O     L B A R
O  S   M   A N I   R I T   N N W   U O   A D L O
G  A   A   N D P   I E H N F   R   N M   L R L W
I  W   L   D A     E P L O F O T   S C   L A   N
S      L   R I T   A   E R M I G   E E R O C K E
T  D   R   E D S T      Y C G L I   L T L E   D
       E   G       T    N A I U V   O A   L   S
       G   I            O M N R E   R N   E   D
       I   T            M I G E     T D   R   N
S C O U T S M           E V E       E     E   E
         D O O W L E Z A H          R         I  G
N  O B O D Y   N O S R E F F E J              R
T  E A C H E R         S   D R A W O C         F
```

ABUSE   COUNSELOR   HAZELWOOD   NOTHING   TALENT

ALCOHOL   COWARD   HOMICIDE   PAIN   TEACHER

ANDREW   DIE   JEFFERSON   POEM   THREE

BANDAIDS   DRAPER   KEISHA   PRAY   TIGER

BASKETBALL   DREAM   LAW   PSYCHOLOGIST   TYRONE

BJ   DROWNED   LETTER   RACE   US

BLACK   FAILURE   MACBETH   RHONDA   WALL

CAPTAIN   FORGIVENESS   MALL   RIPLEY   WASHINGTON

CEILING   FRIENDS   MONTY   ROB   WINTERS

COLD   GERALD   MOVIES   ROCK

COLLEGE   GRAVE   NOBODY   SCOUTS

Tears Of A Tiger Word Search 4

```
W Q P N U G T O H S J E F F E R S O N M
P A I R O R K M Y F V C S H G E C D T M
C A S M A T Q B O M K C N G B T B C Y B
P O Y H A Y H B O N D A I D S T D A R B
V Y U R I L B I S G T R A L M E D H O Y
S L Q N P N L E N H G Y T M V L O S N Q
M C P G S H G T M G A D P P M N L I E Q
D M O V I E S T E K R L A A D D R E A M
Y R C U L X L H O A P Y C A R Z W K N F
W K O L T R H O W N C B B O Y I S R A S
N I O W Y S C O R A E H H F H D P I K X
D C N Z N R C M Z T B E E F H O L L B G
D T V T F E Y T H L D U D R F U L J E J
N A M C E L D V L I Q K S I R R L R M Y
O L L E N R S H C G R A V E B L A C K T
B E W I F D S L K J P N N H L W C H H
O N L L R L M R J R Q D J D D P M R E L
D T S I G O L O H C Y S P S R O E S B P
Y I G N H C C D R W P C N F O E U Q J H
X R E G I T Q K D R A P E R B M W A L L
```

ABUSE	COWARD	KEISHA	PRAY	THREE
ALCOHOL	DIE	LAW	PSYCHOLOGIST	TIGER
ANDREW	DRAPER	LETTER	RACE	TYRONE
BANDAIDS	DREAM	MACBETH	RHONDA	US
BJ	DROWNED	MALL	RIPLEY	WALL
BLACK	FAILURE	MONTY	ROB	WASHINGTON
CAPTAIN	FRIENDS	MOVIES	ROCK	WINTERS
CEILING	GERALD	NOBODY	SCOUTS	
COLD	GRAVE	NOTHING	SHOTGUN	
COLLEGE	HOMICIDE	PAIN	TALENT	
COUNSELOR	JEFFERSON	POEM	TEACHER	

Tears Of A Tiger Word Search 4 Answer Key

```
W   P  N U G T O H S J E F F E R S O N
    A  I R O     M         N         T
C   S  M A T     O         N       E T
P   O  H A Y H B A N D A I D S     T A Y
    U    I L I     T   A     H     T R
S        N N E N   Y   T     M     L O
    C      S G T G A D P     N   O S N
D M O V I E S T E R L A A D R E A M
  R   U    L   L O A   C A R     K     F
W   L  T       O W N C B   O     I     A
    I  O       S   O R A E H     P
    C  N       N   C   T B E F   O     G
    T  T       E   D   H   R U   L     E
N   A  C       E   D       S R R L R   Y
O   L  E       R   C G R A V E B L A C K T
B   E  I       D   S       N N L W C H
O   N  L       R   L M         D P R E
D   T  S         G O L O H C Y S P S R O E S B J
Y      I         N H C C           O E U
       R E G I T       K D R A P E R B M W A L L
```

ABUSE	COWARD	KEISHA	PRAY	THREE
ALCOHOL	DIE	LAW	PSYCHOLOGIST	TIGER
ANDREW	DRAPER	LETTER	RACE	TYRONE
BANDAIDS	DREAM	MACBETH	RHONDA	US
BJ	DROWNED	MALL	RIPLEY	WALL
BLACK	FAILURE	MONTY	ROB	WASHINGTON
CAPTAIN	FRIENDS	MOVIES	ROCK	WINTERS
CEILING	GERALD	NOBODY	SCOUTS	
COLD	GRAVE	NOTHING	SHOTGUN	
COLLEGE	HOMICIDE	PAIN	TALENT	
COUNSELOR	JEFFERSON	POEM	TEACHER	

Tears Of A Tiger Crossword 1

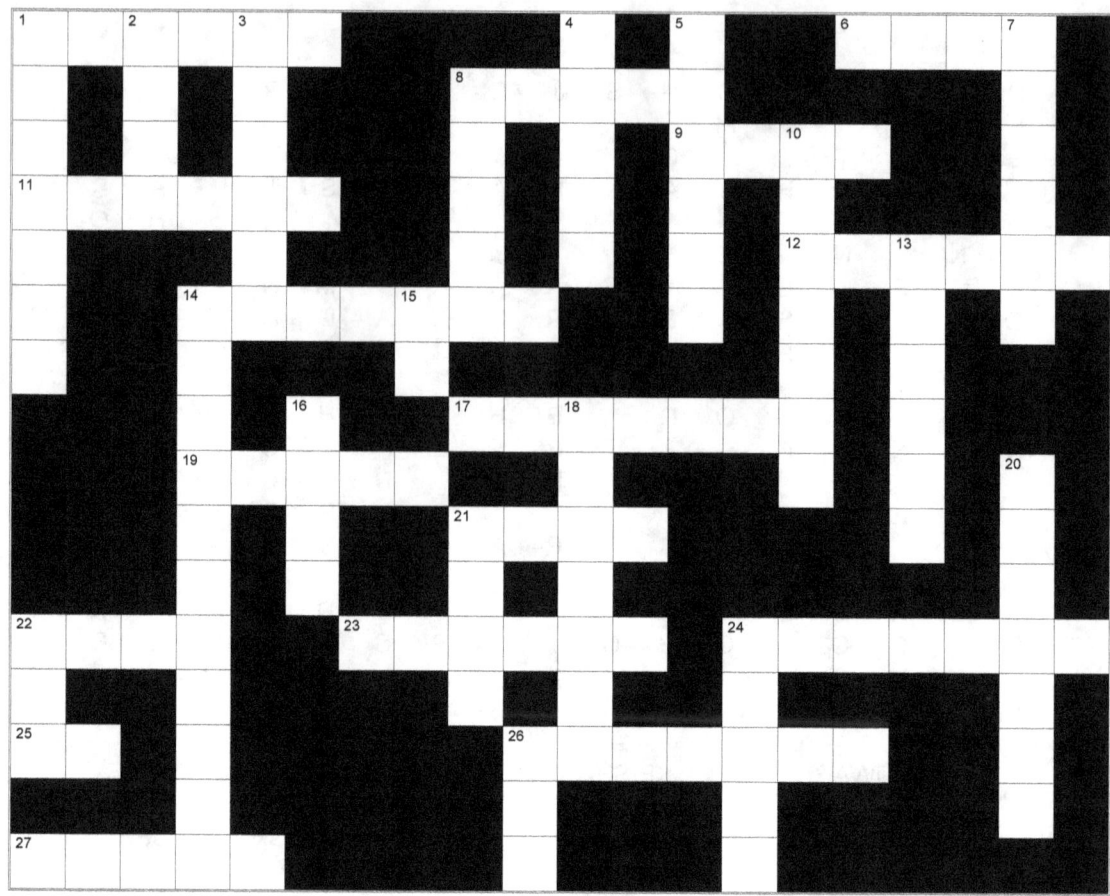

Across
1. Andy's friends think he is a ___ for killing himself.
6. Even though Andy writes this, he doesn't turn it in for a grade.
8. Number of people Andy tries to contact before he kills himself
9. What Rob's mother would always tell Andy he got for Christmas
11. Keisha and Andy break up at the ___ show.
12. Andy sends this to Rob's parents at his psychologist's request.
14. No son of mine is going to be a ___!
17. What Andy says he sees in his future
19. Monty visited Andy there.
21. BJ does this to help cope with the accident.
22. Topic of discussion after reading the snow poem
23. Andy thinks she loves him.
24. Story Andy's class is reading when he runs out of the classroom
25. The only one not drinking the night of the accident
26. Andy tells his mother about a time when he was younger and almost ___.
27. Gerald is a victim of this.

Down
1. Andy gets this position on the team after Rob's death.
2. The car hits this.
3. Keisha's best friend
4. Rob haunts Andy in this.
5. Invited but decides not to go out with the boys after the game
7. Keisha is too busy to go there with Andy.
8. Monty puts tears on this animal.
10. Andy's father dreams of his son going to ___.
13. Helped Andy out of the car
14. Andy asks Rob's parents for this.
15. I knew better. We all did. We just never figured it would happen to __.
16. Keisha is bored with Andy's depression & her mom picks her up there.
18. Andy's father brushes off her concerns.
20. Andy uses this to kill himself.
21. So you're out of it and we have to stay here, feeling your ___ as well as our own.
22. Trapped in the car and burned to death
24. Andy's little brother
26. Rhonda's most frightening moment: realizing that kids could ___

Tears Of A Tiger Crossword 1 Answer Key

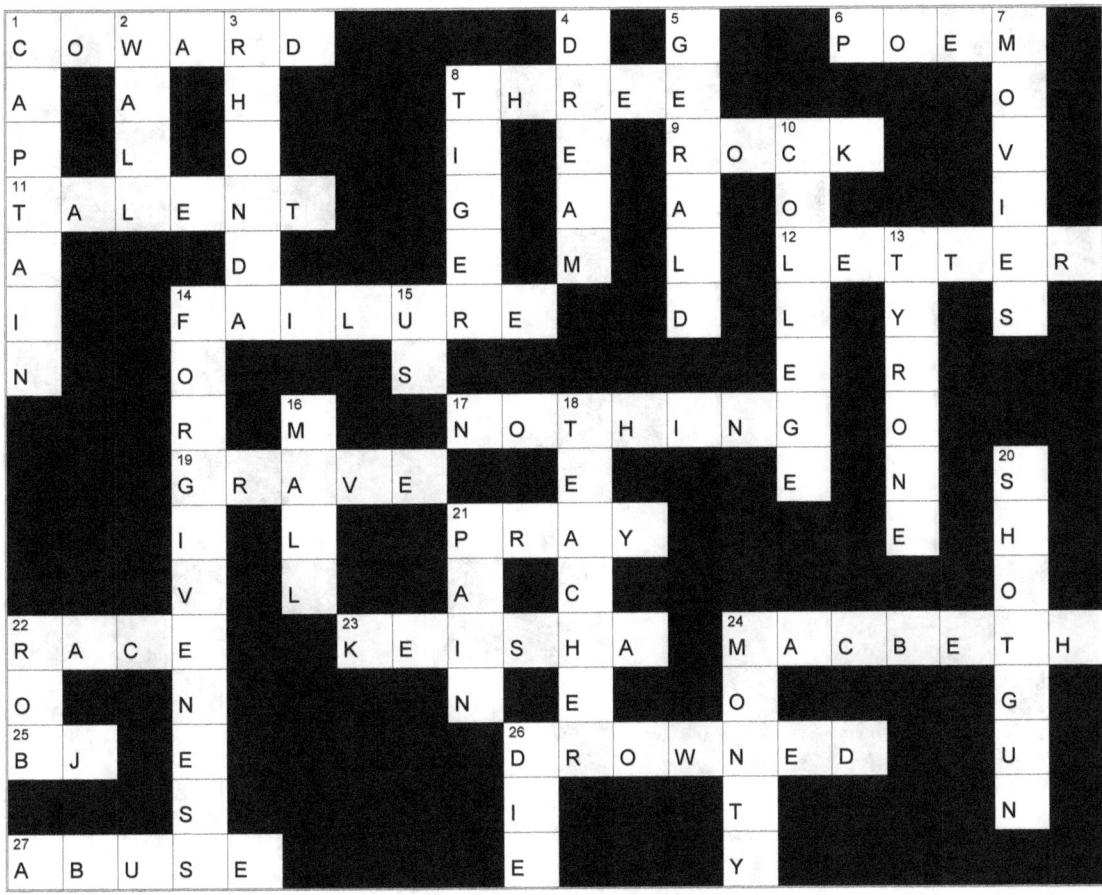

Across
1. Andy's friends think he is a ___ for killing himself.
6. Even though Andy writes this, he doesn't turn it in for a grade.
8. Number of people Andy tries to contact before he kills himself
9. What Rob's mother would always tell Andy he got for Christmas
11. Keisha and Andy break up at the ___ show.
12. Andy sends this to Rob's parents at his psychologist's request.
14. No son of mine is going to be a ___!
17. What Andy says he sees in his future
19. Monty visited Andy there.
21. BJ does this to help cope with the accident.
22. Topic of discussion after reading the snow poem
23. Andy thinks she loves him.
24. Story Andy's class is reading when he runs out of the classroom
25. The only one not drinking the night of the accident
26. Andy tells his mother about a time when he was younger and almost ___.
27. Gerald is a victim of this.

Down
1. Andy gets this position on the team after Rob's death.
2. The car hits this.
3. Keisha's best friend
4. Rob haunts Andy in this.
5. Invited but decides not to go out with the boys after the game
7. Keisha is too busy to go there with Andy.
8. Monty puts tears on this animal.
10. Andy's father dreams of his son going to ___.
13. Helped Andy out of the car
14. Andy asks Rob's parents for this.
15. I knew better. We all did. We just never figured it would happen to __.
16. Keisha is bored with Andy's depression & her mom picks her up there.
18. Andy's father brushes off her concerns.
20. Andy uses this to kill himself.
21. So you're out of it and we have to stay here, feeling your ___ as well as our own.
22. Trapped in the car and burned to death
24. Andy's little brother
26. Rhonda's most frightening moment: realizing that kids could ___

Tears Of A Tiger Crossword 2

Across
1. Rob haunts Andy in this.
2. Invited but decides not to go out with the boys after the game
6. Monty puts tears on this animal.
8. The car hits this.
9. Helped Andy out of the car
10. Story Andy's class is reading when he runs out of the classroom
13. Andy gets this position on the team after Rob's death.
14. Andy sends this to Rob's parents at his psychologist's request.
17. One Thousand Nine Hundred Sixty-Eight ___
18. I knew better. We all did. We just never figured it would happen to __.
19. Andy asks Rob's parents for this.
21. Andy's little brother
23. One teacher thinks all ___ kids are tough.
25. Monty wonders why there is blood on this.
26. BJ and Tyrone go to see this person in hopes of helping Andy.
27. Monty visited Andy there.

Down
1. Rhonda's most frightening moment: realizing that kids could ___
3. Keisha's best friend
4. Andy may want to major in this.
5. Keisha is bored with Andy's depression & her mom picks her up there.
7. Trapped in the car and burned to death
9. Number of people Andy tries to contact before he kills himself
10. Keisha is too busy to go there with Andy.
11. Andy's father dreams of his son going to ___.
12. Topic of discussion after reading the snow poem
13. Andy's friends think he is a ___ for killing himself.
15. Keisha and Andy break up at the ___ show.
16. Andy thinks she loves him.
19. No son of mine is going to be a ___!
20. What Andy says he sees in his future
22. What Rob's mother would always tell Andy he got for Christmas
24. Andy is worried that Rob will be ___ underground.

Tears Of A Tiger Crossword 2 Answer Key

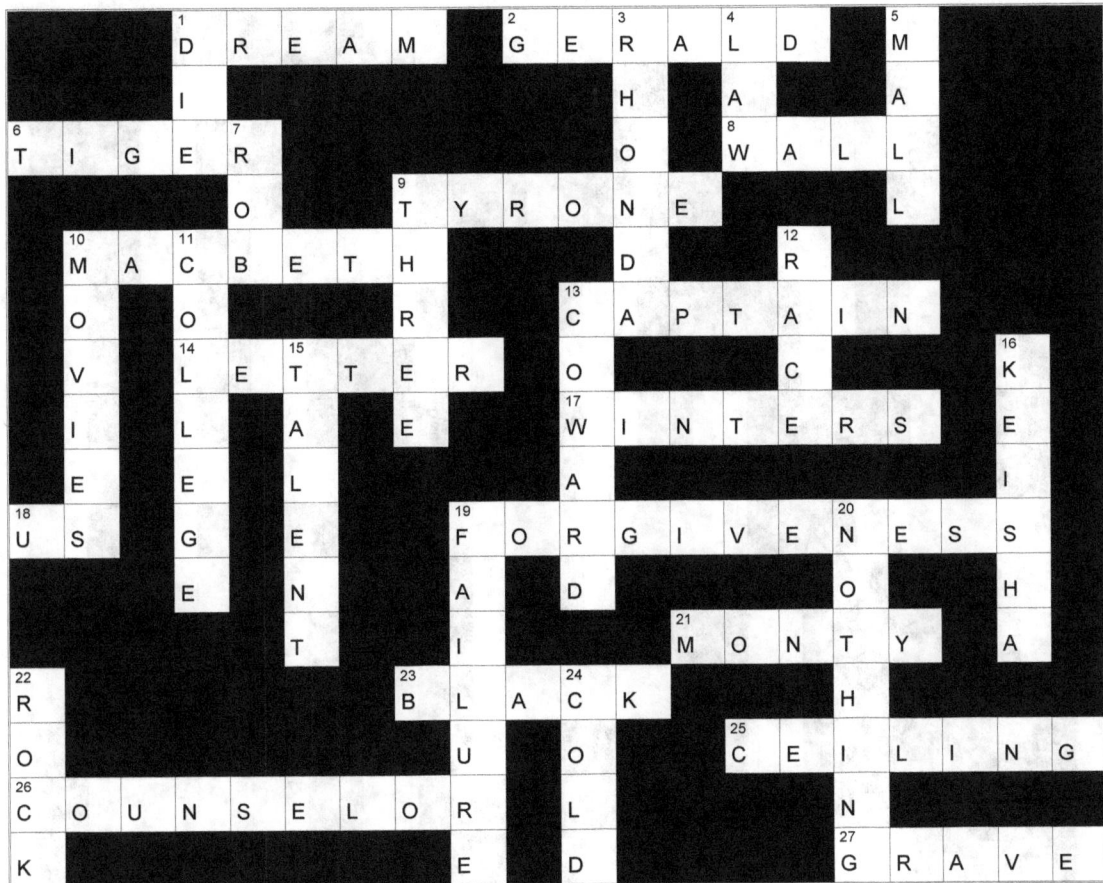

Across
1. Rob haunts Andy in this.
2. Invited but decides not to go out with the boys after the game
6. Monty puts tears on this animal.
8. The car hits this.
9. Helped Andy out of the car
10. Story Andy's class is reading when he runs out of the classroom
13. Andy gets this position on the team after Rob's death.
14. Andy sends this to Rob's parents at his psychologist's request.
17. One Thousand Nine Hundred Sixty-Eight ___
18. I knew better. We all did. We just never figured it would happen to __.
19. Andy asks Rob's parents for this.
21. Andy's little brother
23. One teacher thinks all ___ kids are tough.
25. Monty wonders why there is blood on this.
26. BJ and Tyrone go to see this person in hopes of helping Andy.
27. Monty visited Andy there.

Down
1. Rhonda's most frightening moment: realizing that kids could ___
3. Keisha's best friend
4. Andy may want to major in this.
5. Keisha is bored with Andy's depression & her mom picks her up there.
7. Trapped in the car and burned to death
9. Number of people Andy tries to contact before he kills himself
10. Keisha is too busy to go there with Andy.
11. Andy's father dreams of his son going to ___.
12. Topic of discussion after reading the snow poem
13. Andy's friends think he is a ___ for killing himself.
15. Keisha and Andy break up at the ___ show.
16. Andy thinks she loves him.
19. No son of mine is going to be a ___!
20. What Andy says he sees in his future
22. What Rob's mother would always tell Andy he got for Christmas
24. Andy is worried that Rob will be ___ underground.

Tears Of A Tiger Crossword 3

Across
1. Andy's father did not attend any of these games.
5. What Andy's dad always calls his son
7. Andy's little brother
9. I knew better. We all did. We just never figured it would happen to ___.
11. Monty puts tears on this animal.
12. Monty wonders why there is blood on this.
14. So you're out of it and we have to stay here, feeling your ___ as well as our own.
15. Coach who tried to help Andy
17. Andy sends this to Rob's parents at his psychologist's request.
18. Even though Andy writes this, he doesn't turn it in for a grade.
19. Andy thinks she loves him.
21. Helped Andy out of the car
23. Andy's friends think he is a ___ for killing himself.
25. One teacher thinks all ___ kids are tough.
27. Keisha is bored with Andy's depression & her mom picks her up there.
28. Invited but decides not to go out with the boys after the game

Down
1. The only one not drinking the night of the accident
2. Andy uses this to kill himself.
3. Gerald is a victim of this.
4. Andy may want to major in this.
6. Rob's last name
8. Rhonda's most frightening moment: realizing that kids could ___
10. No son of mine is going to be a ___!
11. Andy's father brushes off her concerns.
12. Andy gets this position on the team after Rob's death.
13. Monty visited Andy there.
15. What Rob's mother would always tell Andy he got for Christmas
16. Keisha's best friend
18. BJ does this to help cope with the accident.
20. Topic of discussion after reading the snow poem
21. Number of people Andy tries to contact before he kills himself
22. Trapped in the car and burned to death
24. The car hits this.
26. Andy is worried that Rob will be ___ underground.

Tears Of A Tiger Crossword 3 Answer Key

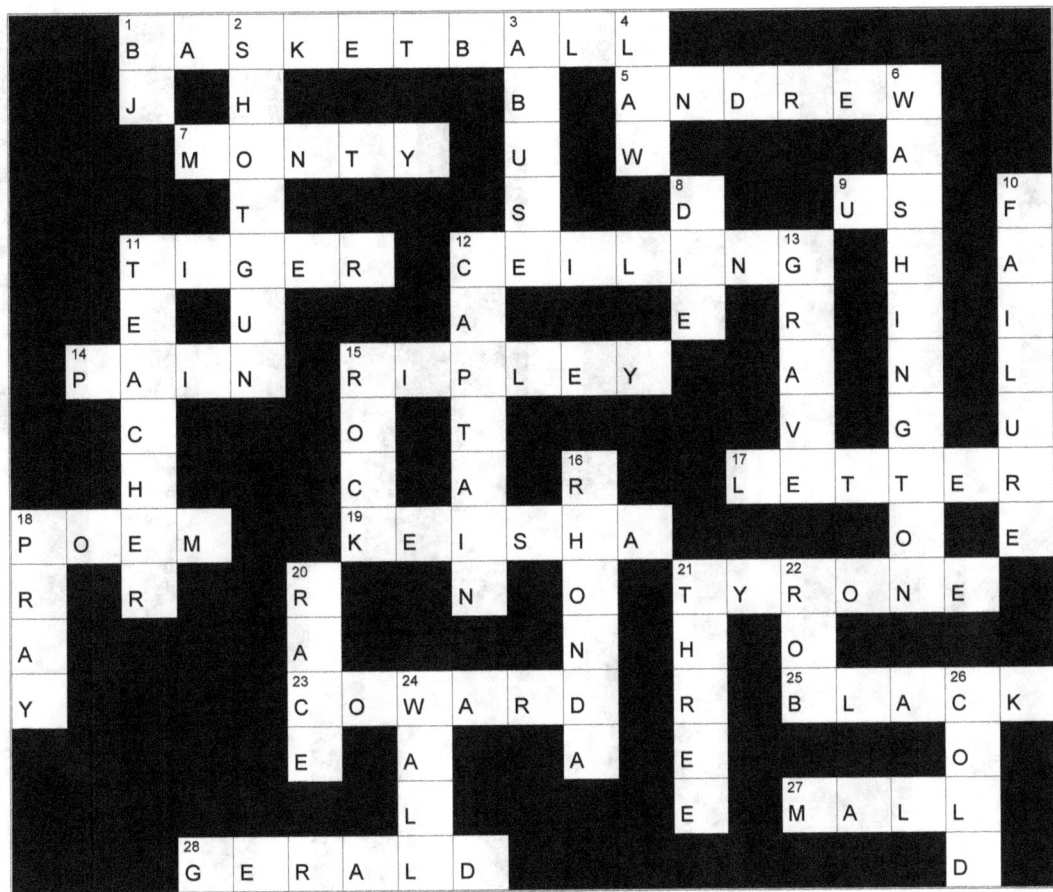

Across
1. Andy's father did not attend any of these games.
5. What Andy's dad always calls his son
7. Andy's little brother
9. I knew better. We all did. We just never figured it would happen to ___.
11. Monty puts tears on this animal.
12. Monty wonders why there is blood on this.
14. So you're out of it and we have to stay here, feeling your ___ as well as our own.
15. Coach who tried to help Andy
17. Andy sends this to Rob's parents at his psychologist's request.
18. Even though Andy writes this, he doesn't turn it in for a grade.
19. Andy thinks she loves him.
21. Helped Andy out of the car
23. Andy's friends think he is a ___ for killing himself.
25. One teacher thinks all ___ kids are tough.
27. Keisha is bored with Andy's depression & her mom picks her up there.
28. Invited but decides not to go out with the boys after the game

Down
1. The only one not drinking the night of the accident
2. Andy uses this to kill himself.
3. Gerald is a victim of this.
4. Andy may want to major in this.
6. Rob's last name
8. Rhonda's most frightening moment: realizing that kids could ___
10. No son of mine is going to be a ___!
11. Andy's father brushes off her concerns.
12. Andy gets this position on the team after Rob's death.
13. Monty visited Andy there.
15. What Rob's mother would always tell Andy he got for Christmas
16. Keisha's best friend
18. BJ does this to help cope with the accident.
20. Topic of discussion after reading the snow poem
21. Number of people Andy tries to contact before he kills himself
22. Trapped in the car and burned to death
24. The car hits this.
26. Andy is worried that Rob will be ___ underground.

Tears Of A Tiger Crossword 4

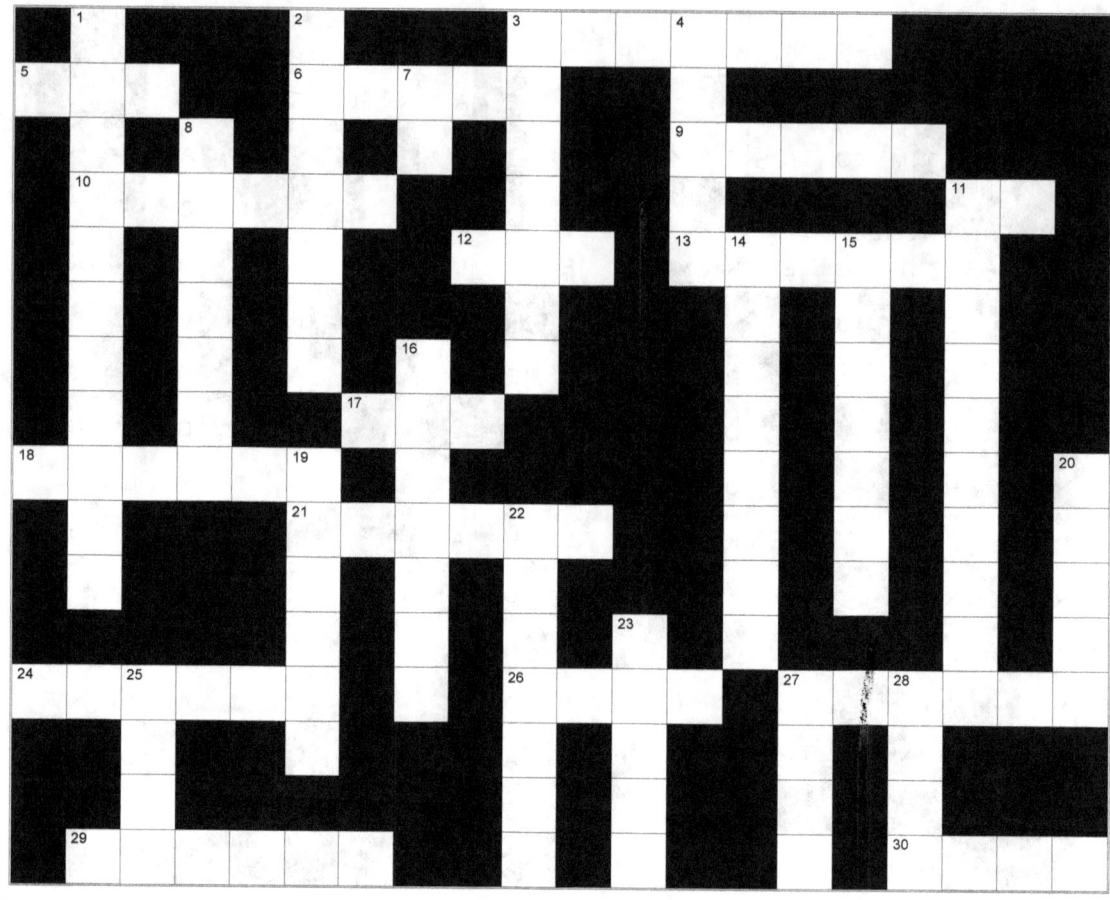

Across
3. Andy gets this position on the team after Rob's death.
5. Trapped in the car and burned to death
6. Gerald is a victim of this.
9. Monty visited Andy there.
10. Invited but decides not to go out with the boys after the game
11. The only one not drinking the night of the accident
12. Rhonda's most frightening moment: realizing that kids could ___
13. Keisha's best friend
17. Andy may want to major in this.
18. Andy thinks she loves him.
21. ___'s home. ___ cares....I wish I could sleep forever.
24. Helped Andy out of the car
26. The car hits this.
27. Coach who tried to help Andy
29. Andy sends this to Rob's parents at his psychologist's request.
30. Keisha is bored with Andy's depression & her mom picks her up there.

Down
1. Andy asks Rob's parents for this.
2. No son of mine is going to be a ___!
3. Monty wonders why there is blood on this.
4. Monty puts tears on this animal.
7. I knew better. We all did. We just never figured it would happen to __.
8. Keisha says life without them would be boring and meaningless.
11. Andy's father did not attend any of these games.
14. Andy is charged with DWI and vehicular ___.
15. What Andy says he sees in his future
16. Story Andy's class is reading when he runs out of the classroom
19. What Andy's dad always calls his son
20. Andy's little brother
22. Andy tells his mother about a time when he was younger and almost ___.
23. One teacher thinks all ___ kids are tough.
25. Topic of discussion after reading the snow poem
27. What Rob's mother would always tell Andy he got for Christmas
28. Even though Andy writes this, he doesn't turn it in for a grade.

Tears Of A Tiger Crossword 4 Answer Key

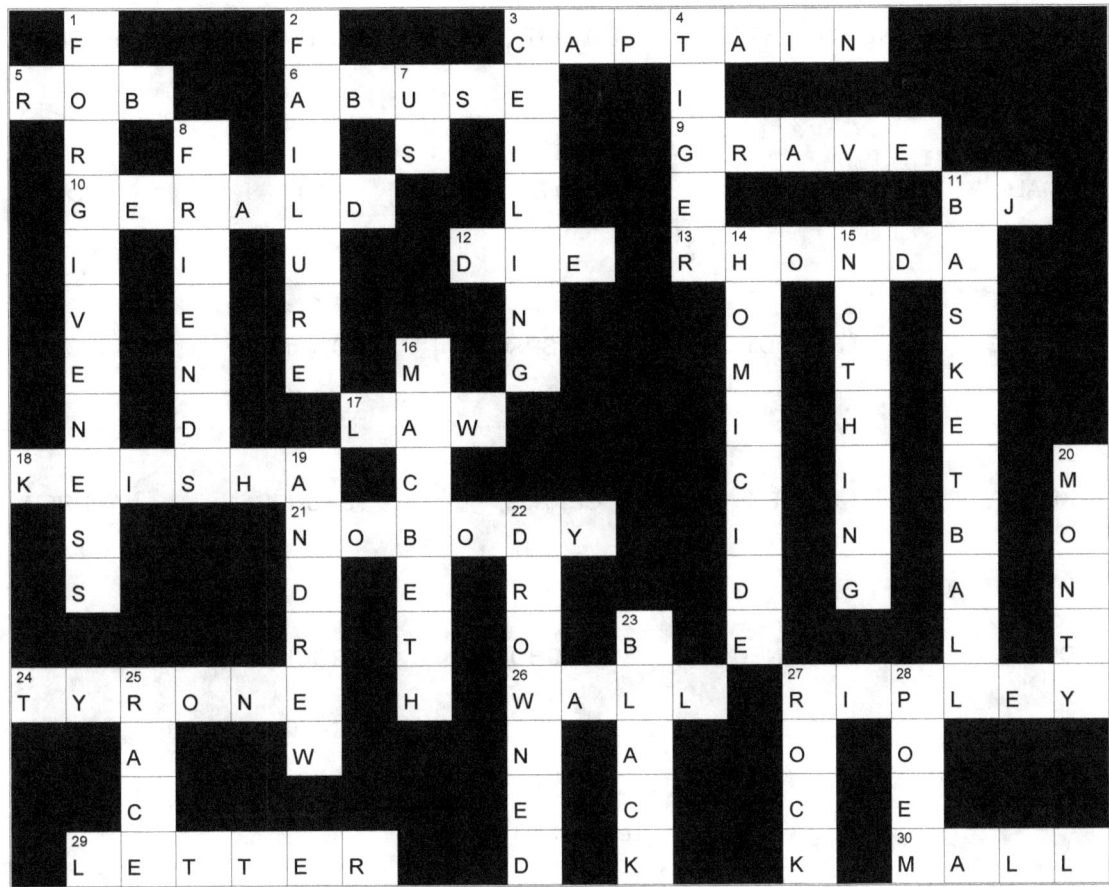

Across
3. Andy gets this position on the team after Rob's death.
5. Trapped in the car and burned to death
6. Gerald is a victim of this.
9. Monty visited Andy there.
10. Invited but decides not to go out with the boys after the game
11. The only one not drinking the night of the accident
12. Rhonda's most frightening moment: realizing that kids could ___
13. Keisha's best friend
17. Andy may want to major in this.
18. Andy thinks she loves him.
21. ___'s home. ___ cares....I wish I could sleep forever.
24. Helped Andy out of the car
26. The car hits this.
27. Coach who tried to help Andy
29. Andy sends this to Rob's parents at his psychologist's request.
30. Keisha is bored with Andy's depression & her mom picks her up there.

Down
1. Andy asks Rob's parents for this.
2. No son of mine is going to be a ___!
3. Monty wonders why there is blood on this.
4. Monty puts tears on this animal.
7. I knew better. We all did. We just never figured it would happen to __.
8. Keisha says life without them would be boring and meaningless.
11. Andy's father did not attend any of these games.
14. Andy is charged with DWI and vehicular ___.
15. What Andy says he sees in his future
16. Story Andy's class is reading when he runs out of the classroom
19. What Andy's dad always calls his son
20. Andy's little brother
22. Andy tells his mother about a time when he was younger and almost ___.
23. One teacher thinks all ___ kids are tough.
25. Topic of discussion after reading the snow poem
27. What Rob's mother would always tell Andy he got for Christmas
28. Even though Andy writes this, he doesn't turn it in for a grade.

Tears Of A Tiger

TYRONE	LETTER	MONTY	WINTERS	RHONDA
MALL	US	DIE	BJ	COLD
GRAVE	NOBODY	FREE SPACE	COWARD	BANDAIDS
KEISHA	MOVIES	GERALD	TEACHER	ANDREW
DREAM	DROWNED	ALCOHOL	ROCK	CEILING

Tears Of A Tiger

CAPTAIN	DRAPER	RACE	BASKETBALL	THREE
PAIN	POEM	TALENT	SCOUTS	JEFFERSON
ABUSE	MACBETH	FREE SPACE	ROB	FRIENDS
PSYCHOLOGIST	LAW	SHOTGUN	NOTHING	TIGER
HOMICIDE	FAILURE	COUNSELOR	BLACK	RIPLEY

Tears Of A Tiger

LAW	ANDREW	JEFFERSON	TYRONE	FRIENDS
ABUSE	COWARD	BJ	BLACK	RIPLEY
HAZELWOOD	MOVIES	FREE SPACE	LETTER	DRAPER
DROWNED	MALL	MONTY	PSYCHOLOGIST	GRAVE
MACBETH	RACE	COLD	TALENT	CEILING

Tears Of A Tiger

BANDAIDS	FAILURE	POEM	TEACHER	TIGER
WINTERS	ROCK	KEISHA	COLLEGE	NOTHING
BASKETBALL	PRAY	FREE SPACE	GERALD	WASHINGTON
US	COUNSELOR	DREAM	THREE	RHONDA
FORGIVENESS	SCOUTS	CAPTAIN	DIE	SHOTGUN

Tears Of A Tiger

SCOUTS	PAIN	COUNSELOR	JEFFERSON	PSYCHOLOGIST
BLACK	TIGER	MONTY	NOTHING	RHONDA
POEM	BJ	FREE SPACE	FRIENDS	RIPLEY
MACBETH	GERALD	DIE	PRAY	CAPTAIN
HOMICIDE	WINTERS	FORGIVENESS	BASKETBALL	ABUSE

Tears Of A Tiger

RACE	FAILURE	COWARD	CEILING	TEACHER
DREAM	ALCOHOL	US	MOVIES	LAW
GRAVE	HAZELWOOD	FREE SPACE	ROCK	DROWNED
TYRONE	ROB	COLD	LETTER	COLLEGE
BANDAIDS	MALL	THREE	KEISHA	WALL

Tears Of A Tiger

ROB	RIPLEY	MALL	CAPTAIN	ANDREW
LETTER	COUNSELOR	WALL	PRAY	GRAVE
US	COLD	FREE SPACE	LAW	MONTY
ROCK	DREAM	WASHINGTON	PSYCHOLOGIST	RACE
JEFFERSON	MACBETH	CEILING	HOMICIDE	POEM

Tears Of A Tiger

FAILURE	NOBODY	BASKETBALL	KEISHA	SCOUTS
ABUSE	HAZELWOOD	BJ	TEACHER	PAIN
GERALD	FRIENDS	FREE SPACE	FORGIVENESS	BLACK
TALENT	DIE	TIGER	COLLEGE	SHOTGUN
COWARD	THREE	BANDAIDS	DRAPER	ALCOHOL

Tears Of A Tiger

DIE	PRAY	WINTERS	KEISHA	WASHINGTON
MACBETH	BASKETBALL	COLLEGE	TALENT	DRAPER
TYRONE	RACE	FREE SPACE	LETTER	COLD
COWARD	NOTHING	POEM	MOVIES	TEACHER
ROB	LAW	PAIN	BLACK	FAILURE

Tears Of A Tiger

ROCK	RHONDA	NOBODY	THREE	ANDREW
CAPTAIN	RIPLEY	GRAVE	BJ	BANDAIDS
SCOUTS	ALCOHOL	FREE SPACE	GERALD	JEFFERSON
US	CEILING	HAZELWOOD	HOMICIDE	MONTY
FORGIVENESS	DREAM	MALL	TIGER	FRIENDS

Tears Of A Tiger

WASHINGTON	MOVIES	JEFFERSON	COWARD	NOTHING
ABUSE	KEISHA	ALCOHOL	PSYCHOLOGIST	MALL
BANDAIDS	RACE	FREE SPACE	PRAY	LETTER
TALENT	BASKETBALL	SCOUTS	BJ	NOBODY
GRAVE	TIGER	FRIENDS	DROWNED	HAZELWOOD

Tears Of A Tiger

CEILING	DIE	COLLEGE	HOMICIDE	ANDREW
THREE	WINTERS	MONTY	US	COUNSELOR
RHONDA	MACBETH	FREE SPACE	TEACHER	COLD
TYRONE	SHOTGUN	POEM	PAIN	BLACK
RIPLEY	ROB	FORGIVENESS	ROCK	GERALD

Tears Of A Tiger

TALENT	PAIN	RACE	RHONDA	BLACK
US	COLD	MACBETH	PSYCHOLOGIST	BANDAIDS
HAZELWOOD	GRAVE	FREE SPACE	KEISHA	BJ
GERALD	COWARD	ALCOHOL	SCOUTS	COUNSELOR
CAPTAIN	FAILURE	MOVIES	TIGER	LETTER

Tears Of A Tiger

FRIENDS	NOTHING	POEM	DRAPER	ABUSE
LAW	MALL	DROWNED	PRAY	NOBODY
THREE	WINTERS	FREE SPACE	ROB	DIE
TEACHER	BASKETBALL	DREAM	FORGIVENESS	SHOTGUN
WALL	COLLEGE	JEFFERSON	HOMICIDE	RIPLEY

Tears Of A Tiger

TEACHER	CEILING	BLACK	ROB	GRAVE
BANDAIDS	JEFFERSON	RACE	TYRONE	PRAY
PSYCHOLOGIST	NOTHING	FREE SPACE	KEISHA	SHOTGUN
DROWNED	WINTERS	FAILURE	LETTER	COLD
WALL	COWARD	DIE	POEM	COLLEGE

Tears Of A Tiger

MOVIES	RHONDA	TALENT	LAW	HAZELWOOD
US	FRIENDS	GERALD	MALL	COUNSELOR
TIGER	PAIN	FREE SPACE	ABUSE	ALCOHOL
FORGIVENESS	THREE	DRAPER	SCOUTS	BJ
BASKETBALL	ANDREW	CAPTAIN	MACBETH	WASHINGTON

Tears Of A Tiger

NOBODY	MONTY	ANDREW	PAIN	RIPLEY
PRAY	DREAM	BJ	DROWNED	TEACHER
FRIENDS	KEISHA	FREE SPACE	WALL	WASHINGTON
SHOTGUN	GERALD	COUNSELOR	NOTHING	MACBETH
TALENT	SCOUTS	FORGIVENESS	FAILURE	BANDAIDS

Tears Of A Tiger

BASKETBALL	RHONDA	TIGER	ROB	US
CAPTAIN	COLLEGE	WINTERS	ROCK	CEILING
DRAPER	COWARD	FREE SPACE	GRAVE	HAZELWOOD
LETTER	DIE	MALL	JEFFERSON	TYRONE
RACE	MOVIES	ALCOHOL	POEM	ABUSE

Tears Of A Tiger

WASHINGTON	MACBETH	TYRONE	ROCK	MALL
ABUSE	TIGER	COWARD	WINTERS	RIPLEY
DREAM	ALCOHOL	FREE SPACE	SHOTGUN	KEISHA
WALL	MOVIES	COLLEGE	THREE	HAZELWOOD
LAW	DIE	ROB	GRAVE	CEILING

Tears Of A Tiger

SCOUTS	TALENT	HOMICIDE	BASKETBALL	DRAPER
ANDREW	US	CAPTAIN	LETTER	BJ
PSYCHOLOGIST	COLD	FREE SPACE	RHONDA	NOTHING
PAIN	MONTY	FRIENDS	DROWNED	COUNSELOR
GERALD	FORGIVENESS	BANDAIDS	JEFFERSON	POEM

Tears Of A Tiger

MOVIES	COUNSELOR	BJ	FRIENDS	ROB
FAILURE	SCOUTS	NOBODY	COWARD	CAPTAIN
ROCK	TEACHER	FREE SPACE	RHONDA	PRAY
CEILING	LAW	ALCOHOL	SHOTGUN	MALL
WINTERS	MONTY	FORGIVENESS	THREE	BANDAIDS

Tears Of A Tiger

LETTER	COLD	WASHINGTON	TIGER	RIPLEY
TYRONE	GRAVE	DROWNED	TALENT	ANDREW
ABUSE	BLACK	FREE SPACE	NOTHING	US
COLLEGE	HAZELWOOD	KEISHA	BASKETBALL	DREAM
HOMICIDE	GERALD	WALL	DRAPER	POEM

Tears Of A Tiger

COWARD	FRIENDS	BJ	FORGIVENESS	DROWNED
US	SCOUTS	BLACK	TEACHER	RIPLEY
RACE	COLLEGE	FREE SPACE	TIGER	ABUSE
ANDREW	PRAY	KEISHA	DREAM	FAILURE
SHOTGUN	COLD	NOBODY	COUNSELOR	BASKETBALL

Tears Of A Tiger

DRAPER	CEILING	CAPTAIN	JEFFERSON	ALCOHOL
NOTHING	THREE	MOVIES	GERALD	LAW
POEM	TYRONE	FREE SPACE	PAIN	HAZELWOOD
TALENT	MONTY	WASHINGTON	HOMICIDE	BANDAIDS
MALL	ROB	ROCK	DIE	WINTERS

Tears Of A Tiger

POEM	BANDAIDS	LAW	JEFFERSON	KEISHA
RHONDA	ALCOHOL	US	NOBODY	BLACK
GERALD	PRAY	FREE SPACE	WINTERS	DRAPER
NOTHING	PSYCHOLOGIST	THREE	FRIENDS	ABUSE
DREAM	TALENT	WALL	MOVIES	CAPTAIN

Tears Of A Tiger

DROWNED	WASHINGTON	ROB	RIPLEY	FAILURE
SCOUTS	TYRONE	LETTER	ANDREW	HAZELWOOD
GRAVE	BJ	FREE SPACE	PAIN	TEACHER
MONTY	COLD	TIGER	CEILING	RACE
DIE	COWARD	COUNSELOR	FORGIVENESS	MACBETH

Tears Of A Tiger

POEM	PSYCHOLOGIST	SCOUTS	US	PRAY
DRAPER	GRAVE	PAIN	ABUSE	NOBODY
COLLEGE	ROCK	FREE SPACE	MALL	COUNSELOR
BJ	FRIENDS	DIE	TYRONE	SHOTGUN
HOMICIDE	THREE	TALENT	MACBETH	BLACK

Tears Of A Tiger

WASHINGTON	DREAM	FORGIVENESS	WALL	TEACHER
CAPTAIN	FAILURE	LETTER	GERALD	HAZELWOOD
MOVIES	TIGER	FREE SPACE	BANDAIDS	LAW
WINTERS	BASKETBALL	RACE	CEILING	ROB
MONTY	KEISHA	RHONDA	ALCOHOL	COLD

Tears Of A Tiger

MACBETH	HAZELWOOD	JEFFERSON	POEM	CEILING
CAPTAIN	RHONDA	COWARD	GRAVE	ROCK
NOBODY	US	FREE SPACE	LETTER	PRAY
SCOUTS	COUNSELOR	SHOTGUN	TEACHER	GERALD
ANDREW	FRIENDS	NOTHING	LAW	BLACK

Tears Of A Tiger

WASHINGTON	TALENT	ROB	DIE	WINTERS
TIGER	WALL	RACE	DREAM	MOVIES
COLLEGE	COLD	FREE SPACE	KEISHA	PAIN
FAILURE	ABUSE	FORGIVENESS	BANDAIDS	RIPLEY
THREE	BJ	HOMICIDE	PSYCHOLOGIST	MALL

Tears Of A Tiger

WINTERS	FAILURE	CEILING	DROWNED	POEM
COWARD	DRAPER	NOTHING	BLACK	SCOUTS
PRAY	ALCOHOL	FREE SPACE	ROB	SHOTGUN
PSYCHOLOGIST	WASHINGTON	LETTER	RIPLEY	TYRONE
COUNSELOR	GRAVE	TIGER	DREAM	WALL

Tears Of A Tiger

HAZELWOOD	DIE	RHONDA	FORGIVENESS	GERALD
BASKETBALL	RACE	PAIN	LAW	HOMICIDE
ABUSE	NOBODY	FREE SPACE	ROCK	TEACHER
FRIENDS	MACBETH	BANDAIDS	ANDREW	KEISHA
MOVIES	TALENT	US	CAPTAIN	MALL

Tears Of A Tiger Vocabulary Word List

No.	Word	Clue/Definition
1.	ACCUSTOMED	In the habit of; used to
2.	APPARENT	Easily perceived or understood
3.	ASPECTS	Parts; features; phases
4.	ASSET	A useful and desirable thing or quality
5.	ASSIMILATE	Become a part of the main or dominant culture
6.	ASSURED	Guaranteed; for sure; certain
7.	BOMBARD	To attack or assail, as with artillery or rapid fire
8.	CAPABLE	Having the ability
9.	COMMODITIES	Articles of trade or commerce; products
10.	CONFIDENCES	Feelings of assurance that a secret will be kept
11.	CONVERT	Persuade to adopt a particular belief
12.	CYNICAL	Distrusting or seeing the worst in the motives of others
13.	DENSE	Difficult to understand or follow because of being closely packed with ideas or complex styles
14.	DESIRE	A longing for; wanting
15.	DETERIORATION	The process of growing worse, weakening, or declining
16.	DETRIMENT	A cause of loss, damage, disadvantage, or injury
17.	DIALECT	Regional or social variety of a language
18.	DISPENSE	Deal out; distribute
19.	DISTURBANCES	Outbreaks of disorder; commotion
20.	ELIMINATE	Get rid of; remove
21.	FORTUNATE	Lucky
22.	FRENZIED	Wildly excited or enthusiastic
23.	GENUINELY	Actually; really; authentically
24.	GRIEVING	Experiencing or expressing sorrow
25.	HECTIC	Characterized by intense activity, confusion, or haste
26.	HONORABLE	Deserving or winning respect or distinction
27.	IMPLANTS	Sets securely in place
28.	INCIDENTS	Minor events
29.	INEVITABLE	Unable to be avoided or escaped; certain
30.	INFINITE	Immeasurably great or large; boundless
31.	INHIBITIONS	Conscious or unconscious restraint of a behavior
32.	INTENTIONS	Objectives; motives
33.	INTRUDE	Put or force in inappropriately, especially without permission
34.	PATIENT	Having calm endurance
35.	PUNITIVE	Punishing
36.	REBELLIOUS	Going against control or authority
37.	RECUPERATED	Returned to health or strength; recovered
38.	REMARKABLE	Worthy of notice or attention
39.	REPREHENSIBLE	Deserving of reproof, rebuke, or censure; blameworthy
40.	REVELATION	An enlightening or astonishing disclosure
41.	RIGHTEOUS	Acting in an upright, moral way; virtuous
42.	SEVERITY	Intensity or sharpness
43.	SUBSTANTIAL	Of ample or considerable amount
44.	SUICIDE	The act of intentionally killing oneself
45.	TOLERATE	To endure; to put up with
46.	TRIBUTE	An acknowledgment of gratitude, respect, or admiration
47.	UNDIGNIFIED	Lacking respect and honor
48.	UNRULY	Difficult or impossible to discipline or control
49.	VAGUELY	Not clearly; hazily; somewhat
50.	VAST	Very great in area or extent; immense
51.	VERBALIZE	To express in words
52.	VITAL	Of critical importance

Tears Of A Tiger Vocabulary Fill In The Blanks 1

_____ 1. Minor events

_____ 2. Lacking respect and honor

_____ 3. Guaranteed; for sure; certain

_____ 4. Difficult or impossible to discipline or control

_____ 5. Become a part of the main or dominant culture

_____ 6. Not clearly; hazily; somewhat

_____ 7. Worthy of notice or attention

_____ 8. Of critical importance

_____ 9. An acknowledgment of gratitude, respect, or admiration

_____ 10. Easily perceived or understood

_____ 11. Conscious or unconscious restraint of a behavior

_____ 12. Put or force in inappropriately, especially without permission

_____ 13. Deal out; distribute

_____ 14. Difficult to understand or follow because of being closely packed with ideas or complex styles

_____ 15. Of ample or considerable amount

_____ 16. Characterized by intense activity, confusion, or haste

_____ 17. A longing for; wanting

_____ 18. Lucky

_____ 19. Deserving or winning respect or distinction

_____ 20. Intensity or sharpness

Tears Of A Tiger Vocabulary Fill In The Blanks 1 Answer Key

INCIDENTS	1. Minor events
UNDIGNIFIED	2. Lacking respect and honor
ASSURED	3. Guaranteed; for sure; certain
UNRULY	4. Difficult or impossible to discipline or control
ASSIMILATE	5. Become a part of the main or dominant culture
VAGUELY	6. Not clearly; hazily; somewhat
REMARKABLE	7. Worthy of notice or attention
VITAL	8. Of critical importance
TRIBUTE	9. An acknowledgment of gratitude, respect, or admiration
APPARENT	10. Easily perceived or understood
INHIBITIONS	11. Conscious or unconscious restraint of a behavior
INTRUDE	12. Put or force in inappropriately, especially without permission
DISPENSE	13. Deal out; distribute
DENSE	14. Difficult to understand or follow because of being closely packed with ideas or complex styles
SUBSTANTIAL	15. Of ample or considerable amount
HECTIC	16. Characterized by intense activity, confusion, or haste
DESIRE	17. A longing for; wanting
FORTUNATE	18. Lucky
HONORABLE	19. Deserving or winning respect or distinction
SEVERITY	20. Intensity or sharpness

Tears Of A Tiger Vocabulary Fill In The Blanks 2

_____ 1. Parts; features; phases

_____ 2. Conscious or unconscious restraint of a behavior

_____ 3. Outbreaks of disorder; commotion

_____ 4. Acting in an upright, moral way; virtuous

_____ 5. A useful and desirable thing or quality

_____ 6. To attack or assail, as with artillery or rapid fire

_____ 7. Going against control or authority

_____ 8. Minor events

_____ 9. Deal out; distribute

_____ 10. Having the ability

_____ 11. Articles of trade or commerce; products

_____ 12. Having calm endurance

_____ 13. Returned to health or strength; recovered

_____ 14. Immeasurably great or large; boundless

_____ 15. An enlightening or astonishing disclosure

_____ 16. Objectives; motives

_____ 17. Lucky

_____ 18. Persuade to adopt a particular belief

_____ 19. To endure; to put up with

_____ 20. Regional or social variety of a language

Tears Of A Tiger Vocabulary Fill In The Blanks 2 Answer Key

ASPECTS	1. Parts; features; phases
INHIBITIONS	2. Conscious or unconscious restraint of a behavior
DISTURBANCES	3. Outbreaks of disorder; commotion
RIGHTEOUS	4. Acting in an upright, moral way; virtuous
ASSET	5. A useful and desirable thing or quality
BOMBARD	6. To attack or assail, as with artillery or rapid fire
REBELLIOUS	7. Going against control or authority
INCIDENTS	8. Minor events
DISPENSE	9. Deal out; distribute
CAPABLE	10. Having the ability
COMMODITIES	11. Articles of trade or commerce; products
PATIENT	12. Having calm endurance
RECUPERATED	13. Returned to health or strength; recovered
INFINITE	14. Immeasurably great or large; boundless
REVELATION	15. An enlightening or astonishing disclosure
INTENTIONS	16. Objectives; motives
FORTUNATE	17. Lucky
CONVERT	18. Persuade to adopt a particular belief
TOLERATE	19. To endure; to put up with
DIALECT	20. Regional or social variety of a language

Tears Of A Tiger Vocabulary Fill In The Blanks 3

_____ 1. Acting in an upright, moral way; virtuous

_____ 2. Intensity or sharpness

_____ 3. Get rid of; remove

_____ 4. Persuade to adopt a particular belief

_____ 5. Difficult to understand or follow because of being closely packed with ideas or complex styles

_____ 6. Punishing

_____ 7. Unable to be avoided or escaped; certain

_____ 8. A longing for; wanting

_____ 9. Immeasurably great or large; boundless

_____ 10. Actually; really; authentically

_____ 11. Of ample or considerable amount

_____ 12. Put or force in inappropriately, especially without permission

_____ 13. To express in words

_____ 14. An acknowledgment of gratitude, respect, or admiration

_____ 15. Guaranteed; for sure; certain

_____ 16. Deserving of reproof, rebuke, or censure; blameworthy

_____ 17. Deal out; distribute

_____ 18. Parts; features; phases

_____ 19. Regional or social variety of a language

_____ 20. Outbreaks of disorder; commotion

Tears Of A Tiger Vocabulary Fill In The Blanks 3 Answer Key

RIGHTEOUS	1. Acting in an upright, moral way; virtuous
SEVERITY	2. Intensity or sharpness
ELIMINATE	3. Get rid of; remove
CONVERT	4. Persuade to adopt a particular belief
DENSE	5. Difficult to understand or follow because of being closely packed with ideas or complex styles
PUNITIVE	6. Punishing
INEVITABLE	7. Unable to be avoided or escaped; certain
DESIRE	8. A longing for; wanting
INFINITE	9. Immeasurably great or large; boundless
GENUINELY	10. Actually; really; authentically
SUBSTANTIAL	11. Of ample or considerable amount
INTRUDE	12. Put or force in inappropriately, especially without permission
VERBALIZE	13. To express in words
TRIBUTE	14. An acknowledgment of gratitude, respect, or admiration
ASSURED	15. Guaranteed; for sure; certain
REPREHENSIBLE	16. Deserving of reproof, rebuke, or censure; blameworthy
DISPENSE	17. Deal out; distribute
ASPECTS	18. Parts; features; phases
DIALECT	19. Regional or social variety of a language
DISTURBANCES	20. Outbreaks of disorder; commotion

Tears Of A Tiger Vocabulary Fill In The Blanks 4

_____ 1. A longing for; wanting

_____ 2. The act of intentionally killing oneself

_____ 3. Difficult or impossible to discipline or control

_____ 4. Not clearly; hazily; somewhat

_____ 5. Of critical importance

_____ 6. Deal out; distribute

_____ 7. Experiencing or expressing sorrow

_____ 8. Outbreaks of disorder; commotion

_____ 9. Unable to be avoided or escaped; certain

_____ 10. A cause of loss, damage, disadvantage, or injury

_____ 11. Easily perceived or understood

_____ 12. Get rid of; remove

_____ 13. Very great in area or extent; immense

_____ 14. An acknowledgment of gratitude, respect, or admiration

_____ 15. Returned to health or strength; recovered

_____ 16. Lacking respect and honor

_____ 17. Feelings of assurance that a secret will be kept

_____ 18. Intensity or sharpness

_____ 19. Lucky

_____ 20. Worthy of notice or attention

Tears Of A Tiger Vocabulary Fill In The Blanks 4 Answer Key

DESIRE	1. A longing for; wanting
SUICIDE	2. The act of intentionally killing oneself
UNRULY	3. Difficult or impossible to discipline or control
VAGUELY	4. Not clearly; hazily; somewhat
VITAL	5. Of critical importance
DISPENSE	6. Deal out; distribute
GRIEVING	7. Experiencing or expressing sorrow
DISTURBANCES	8. Outbreaks of disorder; commotion
INEVITABLE	9. Unable to be avoided or escaped; certain
DETRIMENT	10. A cause of loss, damage, disadvantage, or injury
APPARENT	11. Easily perceived or understood
ELIMINATE	12. Get rid of; remove
VAST	13. Very great in area or extent; immense
TRIBUTE	14. An acknowledgment of gratitude, respect, or admiration
RECUPERATED	15. Returned to health or strength; recovered
UNDIGNIFIED	16. Lacking respect and honor
CONFIDENCES	17. Feelings of assurance that a secret will be kept
SEVERITY	18. Intensity or sharpness
FORTUNATE	19. Lucky
REMARKABLE	20. Worthy of notice or attention

Tears Of A Tiger Vocabulary Matching 1

___ 1. PATIENT
___ 2. DETRIMENT
___ 3. DISTURBANCES
___ 4. INHIBITIONS
___ 5. IMPLANTS
___ 6. ASSET
___ 7. DENSE
___ 8. CONVERT
___ 9. SUICIDE
___ 10. UNDIGNIFIED
___ 11. VERBALIZE
___ 12. SUBSTANTIAL
___ 13. INTRUDE
___ 14. HONORABLE
___ 15. REVELATION
___ 16. HECTIC
___ 17. CONFIDENCES
___ 18. RIGHTEOUS
___ 19. INFINITE
___ 20. RECUPERATED
___ 21. GRIEVING
___ 22. ASSURED
___ 23. VAST
___ 24. COMMODITIES
___ 25. TRIBUTE

A. A useful and desirable thing or quality
B. Characterized by intense activity, confusion, or haste
C. Sets securely in place
D. Guaranteed; for sure; certain
E. Difficult to understand or follow because of being closely packed with ideas or complex styles
F. Immeasurably great or large; boundless
G. Of ample or considerable amount
H. Feelings of assurance that a secret will be kept
I. Deserving or winning respect or distinction
J. Persuade to adopt a particular belief
K. A cause of loss, damage, disadvantage, or injury
L. The act of intentionally killing oneself
M. Put or force in inappropriately, especially without permission
N. An enlightening or astonishing disclosure
O. Having calm endurance
P. Outbreaks of disorder; commotion
Q. Lacking respect and honor
R. Articles of trade or commerce; products
S. Conscious or unconscious restraint of a behavior
T. Very great in area or extent; immense
U. An acknowledgment of gratitude, respect, or admiration
V. Experiencing or expressing sorrow
W. Acting in an upright, moral way; virtuous
X. To express in words
Y. Returned to health or strength; recovered

Tears Of A Tiger Vocabulary Matching 1 Answer Key

O - 1.	PATIENT	A. A useful and desirable thing or quality
K - 2.	DETRIMENT	B. Characterized by intense activity, confusion, or haste
P - 3.	DISTURBANCES	C. Sets securely in place
S - 4.	INHIBITIONS	D. Guaranteed; for sure; certain
C - 5.	IMPLANTS	E. Difficult to understand or follow because of being closely packed with ideas or complex styles
A - 6.	ASSET	F. Immeasurably great or large; boundless
E - 7.	DENSE	G. Of ample or considerable amount
J - 8.	CONVERT	H. Feelings of assurance that a secret will be kept
L - 9.	SUICIDE	I. Deserving or winning respect or distinction
Q -10.	UNDIGNIFIED	J. Persuade to adopt a particular belief
X -11.	VERBALIZE	K. A cause of loss, damage, disadvantage, or injury
G -12.	SUBSTANTIAL	L. The act of intentionally killing oneself
M -13.	INTRUDE	M. Put or force in inappropriately, especially without permission
I - 14.	HONORABLE	N. An enlightening or astonishing disclosure
N -15.	REVELATION	O. Having calm endurance
B -16.	HECTIC	P. Outbreaks of disorder; commotion
H -17.	CONFIDENCES	Q. Lacking respect and honor
W -18.	RIGHTEOUS	R. Articles of trade or commerce; products
F -19.	INFINITE	S. Conscious or unconscious restraint of a behavior
Y -20.	RECUPERATED	T. Very great in area or extent; immense
V -21.	GRIEVING	U. An acknowledgment of gratitude, respect, or admiration
D -22.	ASSURED	V. Experiencing or expressing sorrow
T -23.	VAST	W. Acting in an upright, moral way; virtuous
R -24.	COMMODITIES	X. To express in words
U -25.	TRIBUTE	Y. Returned to health or strength; recovered

Tears Of A Tiger Vocabulary Matching 2

___ 1. FRENZIED
___ 2. VAST
___ 3. BOMBARD
___ 4. DETERIORATION
___ 5. ASSURED
___ 6. TRIBUTE
___ 7. APPARENT
___ 8. FORTUNATE
___ 9. GENUINELY
___ 10. REPREHENSIBLE
___ 11. REMARKABLE
___ 12. RECUPERATED
___ 13. ELIMINATE
___ 14. VITAL
___ 15. VERBALIZE
___ 16. REBELLIOUS
___ 17. INEVITABLE
___ 18. RIGHTEOUS
___ 19. UNRULY
___ 20. DETRIMENT
___ 21. TOLERATE
___ 22. HONORABLE
___ 23. ASSIMILATE
___ 24. DISPENSE
___ 25. DIALECT

A. Acting in an upright, moral way; virtuous
B. Returned to health or strength; recovered
C. Worthy of notice or attention
D. Very great in area or extent; immense
E. Deserving or winning respect or distinction
F. Lucky
G. Deal out; distribute
H. Unable to be avoided or escaped; certain
I. Deserving of reproof, rebuke, or censure; blameworthy
J. Regional or social variety of a language
K. Become a part of the main or dominant culture
L. Easily perceived or understood
M. To attack or assail, as with artillery or rapid fire
N. Actually; really; authentically
O. To endure; to put up with
P. Of critical importance
Q. Difficult or impossible to discipline or control
R. A cause of loss, damage, disadvantage, or injury
S. Guaranteed; for sure; certain
T. To express in words
U. An acknowledgment of gratitude, respect, or admiration
V. The process of growing worse, weakening, or declining
W. Wildly excited or enthusiastic
X. Get rid of; remove
Y. Going against control or authority

Tears Of A Tiger Vocabulary Matching 2 Answer Key

W - 1. FRENZIED	A. Acting in an upright, moral way; virtuous
D - 2. VAST	B. Returned to health or strength; recovered
M - 3. BOMBARD	C. Worthy of notice or attention
V - 4. DETERIORATION	D. Very great in area or extent; immense
S - 5. ASSURED	E. Deserving or winning respect or distinction
U - 6. TRIBUTE	F. Lucky
L - 7. APPARENT	G. Deal out; distribute
F - 8. FORTUNATE	H. Unable to be avoided or escaped; certain
N - 9. GENUINELY	I. Deserving of reproof, rebuke, or censure; blameworthy
I - 10. REPREHENSIBLE	J. Regional or social variety of a language
C - 11. REMARKABLE	K. Become a part of the main or dominant culture
B - 12. RECUPERATED	L. Easily perceived or understood
X - 13. ELIMINATE	M. To attack or assail, as with artillery or rapid fire
P - 14. VITAL	N. Actually; really; authentically
T - 15. VERBALIZE	O. To endure; to put up with
Y - 16. REBELLIOUS	P. Of critical importance
H - 17. INEVITABLE	Q. Difficult or impossible to discipline or control
A - 18. RIGHTEOUS	R. A cause of loss, damage, disadvantage, or injury
Q - 19. UNRULY	S. Guaranteed; for sure; certain
R - 20. DETRIMENT	T. To express in words
O - 21. TOLERATE	U. An acknowledgment of gratitude, respect, or admiration
E - 22. HONORABLE	V. The process of growing worse, weakening, or declining
K - 23. ASSIMILATE	W. Wildly excited or enthusiastic
G - 24. DISPENSE	X. Get rid of; remove
J - 25. DIALECT	Y. Going against control or authority

Tears Of A Tiger Vocabulary Matching 3

1. SUBSTANTIAL
2. ACCUSTOMED
3. BOMBARD
4. SUICIDE
5. APPARENT
6. PUNITIVE
7. CONVERT
8. VAGUELY
9. TOLERATE
10. DISPENSE
11. RECUPERATED
12. ASSIMILATE
13. ELIMINATE
14. PATIENT
15. COMMODITIES
16. HECTIC
17. REPREHENSIBLE
18. DETRIMENT
19. CONFIDENCES
20. FORTUNATE
21. GENUINELY
22. REBELLIOUS
23. UNRULY
24. FRENZIED
25. CYNICAL

A. Lucky
B. Become a part of the main or dominant culture
C. Going against control or authority
D. Returned to health or strength; recovered
E. Having calm endurance
F. The act of intentionally killing oneself
G. Deal out; distribute
H. Articles of trade or commerce; products
I. Characterized by intense activity, confusion, or haste
J. Feelings of assurance that a secret will be kept
K. To endure; to put up with
L. Actually; really; authentically
M. To attack or assail, as with artillery or rapid fire
N. Punishing
O. A cause of loss, damage, disadvantage, or injury
P. Distrusting or seeing the worst in the motives of others
Q. In the habit of; used to
R. Easily perceived or understood
S. Deserving of reproof, rebuke, or censure; blameworthy
T. Difficult or impossible to discipline or control
U. Get rid of; remove
V. Of ample or considerable amount
W. Not clearly; hazily; somewhat
X. Wildly excited or enthusiastic
Y. Persuade to adopt a particular belief

Tears Of A Tiger Vocabulary Matching 3 Answer Key

V - 1.	SUBSTANTIAL	A.	Lucky
Q - 2.	ACCUSTOMED	B.	Become a part of the main or dominant culture
M - 3.	BOMBARD	C.	Going against control or authority
F - 4.	SUICIDE	D.	Returned to health or strength; recovered
R - 5.	APPARENT	E.	Having calm endurance
N - 6.	PUNITIVE	F.	The act of intentionally killing oneself
Y - 7.	CONVERT	G.	Deal out; distribute
W - 8.	VAGUELY	H.	Articles of trade or commerce; products
K - 9.	TOLERATE	I.	Characterized by intense activity, confusion, or haste
G - 10.	DISPENSE	J.	Feelings of assurance that a secret will be kept
D - 11.	RECUPERATED	K.	To endure; to put up with
B - 12.	ASSIMILATE	L.	Actually; really; authentically
U - 13.	ELIMINATE	M.	To attack or assail, as with artillery or rapid fire
E - 14.	PATIENT	N.	Punishing
H - 15.	COMMODITIES	O.	A cause of loss, damage, disadvantage, or injury
I - 16.	HECTIC	P.	Distrusting or seeing the worst in the motives of others
S - 17.	REPREHENSIBLE	Q.	In the habit of; used to
O - 18.	DETRIMENT	R.	Easily perceived or understood
J - 19.	CONFIDENCES	S.	Deserving of reproof, rebuke, or censure; blameworthy
A - 20.	FORTUNATE	T.	Difficult or impossible to discipline or control
L - 21.	GENUINELY	U.	Get rid of; remove
C - 22.	REBELLIOUS	V.	Of ample or considerable amount
T - 23.	UNRULY	W.	Not clearly; hazily; somewhat
X - 24.	FRENZIED	X.	Wildly excited or enthusiastic
P - 25.	CYNICAL	Y.	Persuade to adopt a particular belief

Tears Of A Tiger Vocabulary Matching 4

___ 1. COMMODITIES
___ 2. PATIENT
___ 3. BOMBARD
___ 4. ASSURED
___ 5. PUNITIVE
___ 6. DESIRE
___ 7. RIGHTEOUS
___ 8. GENUINELY
___ 9. APPARENT
___10. CONVERT
___11. INCIDENTS
___12. ASSIMILATE
___13. DISTURBANCES
___14. FORTUNATE
___15. DENSE
___16. UNRULY
___17. VITAL
___18. INHIBITIONS
___19. REVELATION
___20. GRIEVING
___21. DISPENSE
___22. TRIBUTE
___23. DETRIMENT
___24. ELIMINATE
___25. CONFIDENCES

A. Guaranteed; for sure; certain
B. To attack or assail, as with artillery or rapid fire
C. Difficult to understand or follow because of being closely packed with ideas or complex styles
D. Having calm endurance
E. Actually; really; authentically
F. A cause of loss, damage, disadvantage, or injury
G. Get rid of; remove
H. Lucky
I. Feelings of assurance that a secret will be kept
J. Articles of trade or commerce; products
K. Minor events
L. An enlightening or astonishing disclosure
M. Acting in an upright, moral way; virtuous
N. Outbreaks of disorder; commotion
O. Persuade to adopt a particular belief
P. Become a part of the main or dominant culture
Q. Difficult or impossible to discipline or control
R. Of critical importance
S. Easily perceived or understood
T. An acknowledgment of gratitude, respect, or admiration
U. Deal out; distribute
V. A longing for; wanting
W. Punishing
X. Conscious or unconscious restraint of a behavior
Y. Experiencing or expressing sorrow

Tears Of A Tiger Vocabulary Matching 4 Answer Key

J - 1. COMMODITIES	A.	Guaranteed; for sure; certain
D - 2. PATIENT	B.	To attack or assail, as with artillery or rapid fire
B - 3. BOMBARD	C.	Difficult to understand or follow because of being closely packed with ideas or complex styles
A - 4. ASSURED	D.	Having calm endurance
W - 5. PUNITIVE	E.	Actually; really; authentically
V - 6. DESIRE	F.	A cause of loss, damage, disadvantage, or injury
M - 7. RIGHTEOUS	G.	Get rid of; remove
E - 8. GENUINELY	H.	Lucky
S - 9. APPARENT	I.	Feelings of assurance that a secret will be kept
O - 10. CONVERT	J.	Articles of trade or commerce; products
K - 11. INCIDENTS	K.	Minor events
P - 12. ASSIMILATE	L.	An enlightening or astonishing disclosure
N - 13. DISTURBANCES	M.	Acting in an upright, moral way; virtuous
H - 14. FORTUNATE	N.	Outbreaks of disorder; commotion
C - 15. DENSE	O.	Persuade to adopt a particular belief
Q - 16. UNRULY	P.	Become a part of the main or dominant culture
R - 17. VITAL	Q.	Difficult or impossible to discipline or control
X - 18. INHIBITIONS	R.	Of critical importance
L - 19. REVELATION	S.	Easily perceived or understood
Y - 20. GRIEVING	T.	An acknowledgment of gratitude, respect, or admiration
U - 21. DISPENSE	U.	Deal out; distribute
T - 22. TRIBUTE	V.	A longing for; wanting
F - 23. DETRIMENT	W.	Punishing
G - 24. ELIMINATE	X.	Conscious or unconscious restraint of a behavior
I - 25. CONFIDENCES	Y.	Experiencing or expressing sorrow

Tears Of A Tiger Vocabulary Magic Squares 1

Match the definition with the vocabulary word. Put your answers in the magic squares below. When your answers are correct, all columns and rows will add to the same number.

A. TOLERATE
B. COMMODITIES
C. REPREHENSIBLE
D. CONVERT
E. BOMBARD
F. DIALECT
G. ACCUSTOMED
H. REBELLIOUS
I. APPARENT
J. CONFIDENCES
K. INFINITE
L. DESIRE
M. TRIBUTE
N. ELIMINATE
O. DISPENSE
P. ASSURED

1. Articles of trade or commerce; products
2. In the habit of; used to
3. Immeasurably great or large; boundless
4. Get rid of; remove
5. An acknowledgment of gratitude, respect, or admiration
6. A longing for; wanting
7. Going against control or authority
8. To endure; to put up with
9. Guaranteed; for sure; certain
10. Easily perceived or understood
11. To attack or assail, as with artillery or rapid fire
12. Persuade to adopt a particular belief
13. Deserving of reproof, rebuke, or censure; blameworthy
14. Regional or social variety of a language
15. Feelings of assurance that a secret will be kept
16. Deal out; distribute

A=8	B=1	C=13	D=12
E=11	F=14	G=2	H=7
I=10	J=15	K=3	L=6
M=5	N=4	O=16	P=9

Tears Of A Tiger Vocabulary Magic Squares 1 Answer Key

Match the definition with the vocabulary word. Put your answers in the magic squares below. When your answers are correct, all columns and rows will add to the same number.

A. TOLERATE
B. COMMODITIES
C. REPREHENSIBLE
D. CONVERT
E. BOMBARD
F. DIALECT
G. ACCUSTOMED
H. REBELLIOUS
I. APPARENT
J. CONFIDENCES
K. INFINITE
L. DESIRE
M. TRIBUTE
N. ELIMINATE
O. DISPENSE
P. ASSURED

1. Articles of trade or commerce; products
2. In the habit of; used to
3. Immeasurably great or large; boundless
4. Get rid of; remove
5. An acknowledgment of gratitude, respect, or admiration
6. A longing for; wanting
7. Going against control or authority
8. To endure; to put up with
9. Guaranteed; for sure; certain
10. Easily perceived or understood
11. To attack or assail, as with artillery or rapid fire
12. Persuade to adopt a particular belief
13. Deserving of reproof, rebuke, or censure; blameworthy
14. Regional or social variety of a language
15. Feelings of assurance that a secret will be kept
16. Deal out; distribute

A=8	B=1	C=13	D=12
E=11	F=14	G=2	H=7
I=10	J=15	K=3	L=6
M=5	N=4	O=16	P=9

Tears Of A Tiger Vocabulary Magic Squares 2

Match the definition with the vocabulary word. Put your answers in the magic squares below. When your answers are correct, all columns and rows will add to the same number.

A. GRIEVING
B. SEVERITY
C. INEVITABLE
D. REPREHENSIBLE
E. TRIBUTE
F. CONFIDENCES
G. VAGUELY
H. INFINITE
I. ASSET
J. APPARENT
K. ASSURED
L. CYNICAL
M. UNRULY
N. DETRIMENT
O. INHIBITIONS
P. DISTURBANCES

1. Feelings of assurance that a secret will be kept
2. A useful and desirable thing or quality
3. Conscious or unconscious restraint of a behavior
4. Deserving of reproof, rebuke, or censure; blameworthy
5. Difficult or impossible to discipline or control
6. Intensity or sharpness
7. Immeasurably great or large; boundless
8. Guaranteed; for sure; certain
9. Unable to be avoided or escaped; certain
10. Outbreaks of disorder; commotion
11. Easily perceived or understood
12. An acknowledgment of gratitude, respect, or admiration
13. Distrusting or seeing the worst in the motives of others
14. Not clearly; hazily; somewhat
15. Experiencing or expressing sorrow
16. A cause of loss, damage, disadvantage, or injury

A=	B=	C=	D=
E=	F=	G=	H=
I=	J=	K=	L=
M=	N=	O=	P=

Tears Of A Tiger Vocabulary Magic Squares 2 Answer Key

Match the definition with the vocabulary word. Put your answers in the magic squares below. When your answers are correct, all columns and rows will add to the same number.

A. GRIEVING
B. SEVERITY
C. INEVITABLE
D. REPREHENSIBLE
E. TRIBUTE
F. CONFIDENCES
G. VAGUELY
H. INFINITE
I. ASSET
J. APPARENT
K. ASSURED
L. CYNICAL
M. UNRULY
N. DETRIMENT
O. INHIBITIONS
P. DISTURBANCES

1. Feelings of assurance that a secret will be kept
2. A useful and desirable thing or quality
3. Conscious or unconscious restraint of a behavior
4. Deserving of reproof, rebuke, or censure; blameworthy
5. Difficult or impossible to discipline or control
6. Intensity or sharpness
7. Immeasurably great or large; boundless
8. Guaranteed; for sure; certain
9. Unable to be avoided or escaped; certain
10. Outbreaks of disorder; commotion
11. Easily perceived or understood
12. An acknowledgment of gratitude, respect, or admiration
13. Distrusting or seeing the worst in the motives of others
14. Not clearly; hazily; somewhat
15. Experiencing or expressing sorrow
16. A cause of loss, damage, disadvantage, or injury

A=15	B=6	C=9	D=4
E=12	F=1	G=14	H=7
I=2	J=11	K=8	L=13
M=5	N=16	O=3	P=10

Tears Of A Tiger Vocabulary Magic Squares 3

Match the definition with the vocabulary word. Put your answers in the magic squares below. When your answers are correct, all columns and rows will add to the same number.

A. GRIEVING
B. FORTUNATE
C. INEVITABLE
D. BOMBARD
E. PATIENT
F. REVELATION
G. REBELLIOUS
H. SUICIDE
I. VAST
J. CYNICAL
K. DESIRE
L. ASSET
M. PUNITIVE
N. REPREHENSIBLE
O. INTRUDE
P. VITAL

1. The act of intentionally killing oneself
2. Punishing
3. Lucky
4. A longing for; wanting
5. Distrusting or seeing the worst in the motives of others
6. Unable to be avoided or escaped; certain
7. Of critical importance
8. Having calm endurance
9. Put or force in inappropriately, especially without permission
10. An enlightening or astonishing disclosure
11. Very great in area or extent; immense
12. To attack or assail, as with artillery or rapid fire
13. Experiencing or expressing sorrow
14. A useful and desirable thing or quality
15. Going against control or authority
16. Deserving of reproof, rebuke, or censure; blameworthy

A=	B=	C=	D=
E=	F=	G=	H=
I=	J=	K=	L=
M=	N=	O=	P=

83
Copyrighted

Tears Of A Tiger Vocabulary Magic Squares 3 Answer Key

Match the definition with the vocabulary word. Put your answers in the magic squares below. When your answers are correct, all columns and rows will add to the same number.

A. GRIEVING
B. FORTUNATE
C. INEVITABLE
D. BOMBARD
E. PATIENT
F. REVELATION
G. REBELLIOUS
H. SUICIDE
I. VAST
J. CYNICAL
K. DESIRE
L. ASSET
M. PUNITIVE
N. REPREHENSIBLE
O. INTRUDE
P. VITAL

1. The act of intentionally killing oneself
2. Punishing
3. Lucky
4. A longing for; wanting
5. Distrusting or seeing the worst in the motives of others
6. Unable to be avoided or escaped; certain
7. Of critical importance
8. Having calm endurance
9. Put or force in inappropriately, especially without permission
10. An enlightening or astonishing disclosure
11. Very great in area or extent; immense
12. To attack or assail, as with artillery or rapid fire
13. Experiencing or expressing sorrow
14. A useful and desirable thing or quality
15. Going against control or authority
16. Deserving of reproof, rebuke, or censure; blameworthy

A=13	B=3	C=6	D=12
E=8	F=10	G=15	H=1
I=11	J=5	K=4	L=14
M=2	N=16	O=9	P=7

Tears Of A Tiger Vocabulary Magic Squares 4

Match the definition with the vocabulary word. Put your answers in the magic squares below. When your answers are correct, all columns and rows will add to the same number.

A. TRIBUTE
B. CYNICAL
C. DENSE
D. HECTIC
E. RECUPERATED
F. REMARKABLE
G. TOLERATE
H. ASPECTS
I. VAST
J. PATIENT
K. CAPABLE
L. CONVERT
M. COMMODITIES
N. VITAL
O. UNRULY
P. GENUINELY

1. An acknowledgment of gratitude, respect, or admiration
2. Of critical importance
3. Having calm endurance
4. Returned to health or strength; recovered
5. To endure; to put up with
6. Persuade to adopt a particular belief
7. Actually; really; authentically
8. Difficult to understand or follow because of being closely packed with ideas or complex styles
9. Difficult or impossible to discipline or control
10. Characterized by intense activity, confusion, or haste
11. Parts; features; phases
12. Having the ability
13. Very great in area or extent; immense
14. Worthy of notice or attention
15. Distrusting or seeing the worst in the motives of others
16. Articles of trade or commerce; products

A=	B=	C=	D=
E=	F=	G=	H=
I=	J=	K=	L=
M=	N=	O=	P=

Tears Of A Tiger Vocabulary Magic Squares 4 Answer Key

Match the definition with the vocabulary word. Put your answers in the magic squares below. When your answers are correct, all columns and rows will add to the same number.

A. TRIBUTE
B. CYNICAL
C. DENSE
D. HECTIC
E. RECUPERATED
F. REMARKABLE
G. TOLERATE
H. ASPECTS
I. VAST
J. PATIENT
K. CAPABLE
L. CONVERT
M. COMMODITIES
N. VITAL
O. UNRULY
P. GENUINELY

1. An acknowledgment of gratitude, respect, or admiration
2. Of critical importance
3. Having calm endurance
4. Returned to health or strength; recovered
5. To endure; to put up with
6. Persuade to adopt a particular belief
7. Actually; really; authentically
8. Difficult to understand or follow because of being closely packed with ideas or complex styles
9. Difficult or impossible to discipline or control
10. Characterized by intense activity, confusion, or haste
11. Parts; features; phases
12. Having the ability
13. Very great in area or extent; immense
14. Worthy of notice or attention
15. Distrusting or seeing the worst in the motives of others
16. Articles of trade or commerce; products

A=1	B=15	C=8	D=10
E=4	F=14	G=5	H=11
I=13	J=3	K=12	L=6
M=16	N=2	O=9	P=7

Tears Of A Tiger Vocabulary Word Search 1

```
T C O M M O D I T I E S T R I B U T E D
O M S C A P A B L E M C O N V E R T D D
L B U J P M R E M A R K A B L E R N A F
E H O I Q M H I N H I B I T I O N S G R
R K E M N Y Z R K J C E S N E P S I D D
A M T C B C K C E P I Y I N F I N I T E
T F H H T A I C V V N T N G M K F E R D
E H G O Y I R D F R E N Z I E D D Y F V
J E I N T Q C D E G V L L V C U M Y J S
S T R O S Y W T P N I A A I R A H Y F Q
L A B R T L S U B S T A N T I A L S O Y
T N S A Z U A E D E A S N A I E F U R S
Y I P B H R S S E Y B I Q L N O P I T J
I M P L A N T S S N L T V I T L N C U W
Q I L E E U Z G I U E C U A E W E I N R
F L M D V Z W S R K R N V X S P Q D A C
V E R B A L I Z E X E E S F S T X E T D
P A T I E N T L B G P N D A A Q V C E Z
```

A longing for; wanting (6)
A useful and desirable thing or quality (5)
Acting in an upright, moral way; virtuous (9)
Actually; really; authentically (9)
An acknowledgment of gratitude, respect, or admiration (7)
An enlightening or astonishing disclosure (10)
Articles of trade or commerce; products (11)
Become a part of the main or dominant culture (10)
Characterized by intense activity, confusion, or haste (6)
Conscious or unconscious restraint of a behavior (11)
Deal out; distribute (8)
Deserving or winning respect or distinction (9)
Difficult or impossible to discipline or control (6)
Difficult to understand or follow because of being closely packed with ideas or complex styles (5)
Distrusting or seeing the worst in the motives of others (7)
Get rid of; remove (9)

Guaranteed; for sure; certain (7)
Having calm endurance (7)
Having the ability (7)
Immeasurably great or large; boundless (8)
Lucky (9)
Minor events (9)
Of ample or considerable amount (11)
Of critical importance (5)
Parts; features; phases (7)
Persuade to adopt a particular belief (7)
Put or force in inappropriately, especially without permission (7)
Sets securely in place (8)
The act of intentionally killing oneself (7)
To attack or assail, as with artillery or rapid fire (7)
To endure; to put up with (8)
To express in words (9)
Unable to be avoided or escaped; certain (10)
Very great in area or extent; immense (4)
Wildly excited or enthusiastic (8)
Worthy of notice or attention (10)

Tears Of A Tiger Vocabulary Word Search 1 Answer Key

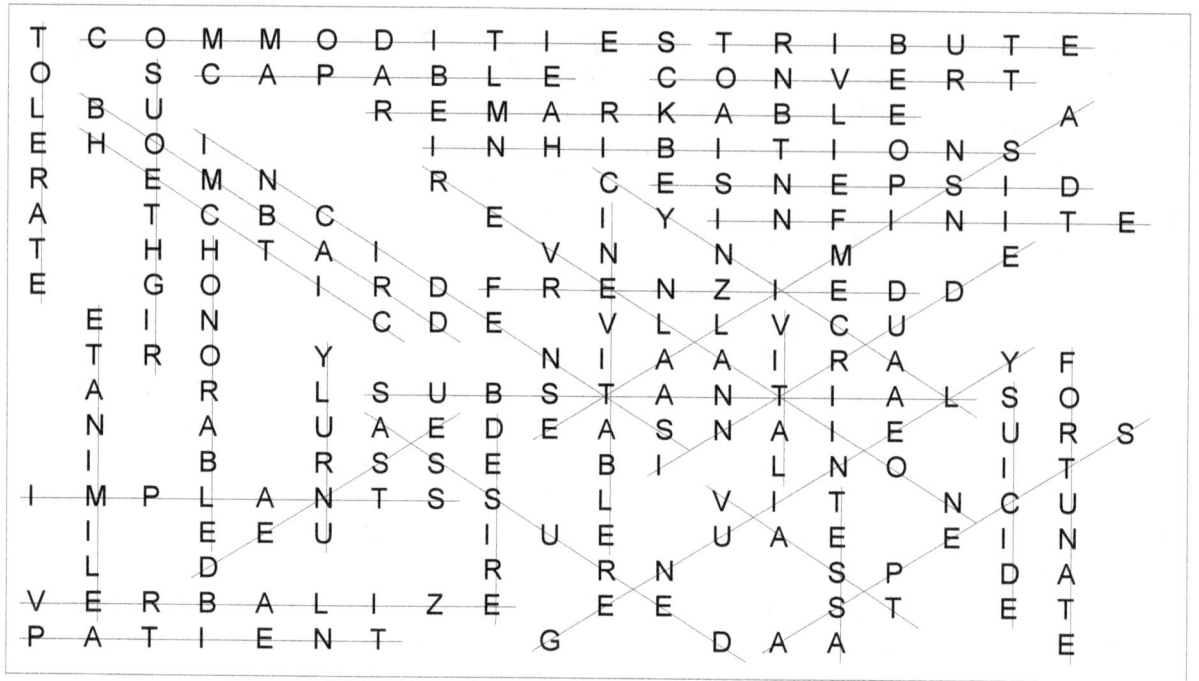

A longing for; wanting (6)
A useful and desirable thing or quality (5)
Acting in an upright, moral way; virtuous (9)
Actually; really; authentically (9)
An acknowledgment of gratitude, respect, or admiration (7)
An enlightening or astonishing disclosure (10)
Articles of trade or commerce; products (11)
Become a part of the main or dominant culture (10)
Characterized by intense activity, confusion, or haste (6)
Conscious or unconscious restraint of a behavior (11)
Deal out; distribute (8)
Deserving or winning respect or distinction (9)
Difficult or impossible to discipline or control (6)
Difficult to understand or follow because of being closely packed with ideas or complex styles (5)
Distrusting or seeing the worst in the motives of others (7)
Get rid of; remove (9)

Guaranteed; for sure; certain (7)
Having calm endurance (7)
Having the ability (7)
Immeasurably great or large; boundless (8)
Lucky (9)
Minor events (9)
Of ample or considerable amount (11)
Of critical importance (5)
Parts; features; phases (7)
Persuade to adopt a particular belief (7)
Put or force in inappropriately, especially without permission (7)
Sets securely in place (8)
The act of intentionally killing oneself (7)
To attack or assail, as with artillery or rapid fire (7)
To endure; to put up with (8)
To express in words (9)
Unable to be avoided or escaped; certain (10)
Very great in area or extent; immense (4)
Wildly excited or enthusiastic (8)
Worthy of notice or attention (10)

Tears Of A Tiger Vocabulary Word Search 2

```
C O M M O D I T I E S U O E T H G I R S
I M P L A N T S T B T S T T E B T G J P
H O N O R A B L E D C M N A L Y G Z C K
U N R U L Y Y C E T E V E R B A L I Z E
S U I C I D E M N L P R R E A M V T F C
E R X T Z P O E B L S A A L P K Z R O L
L K E Y G T M A S N A S P O A I E N Q N
I K C P S I K E O S D S P T C N V X T H
M Q L U R R V I X B E U A G Z E N N V V
I F C T A E T R N S I R X I R V E D I S
N C E M R I H D N K F E E T E I S I T S
A D E I B T C E L A I D V T T T K N A C
T R T I R E P S N M N A U A S A W F L F
E Y H W R S K I X S G B P A S B H I D F
R N F H I S L R S U I C V Q Q L J N E H
I X H D G A N E E R D B G R I E V I N G
C Y N I C A L L T K N J L D D J S T S W
H E C T I C Y G E N U I N E L Y G E E B
```

A cause of loss, damage, disadvantage, or injury (9)
A longing for; wanting (6)
A useful and desirable thing or quality (5)
Acting in an upright, moral way; virtuous (9)
Actually; really; authentically (9)
An acknowledgment of gratitude, respect, or admiration (7)
Articles of trade or commerce; products (11)
Characterized by intense activity, confusion, or haste (6)
Conscious or unconscious restraint of a behavior (11)
Deal out; distribute (8)
Deserving of reproof, rebuke, or censure; blameworthy (13)
Deserving or winning respect or distinction (9)
Difficult or impossible to discipline or control (6)
Difficult to understand or follow because of being closely packed with ideas or complex styles (5)
Distrusting or seeing the worst in the motives of others (7)
Easily perceived or understood (8)
Experiencing or expressing sorrow (8)
Get rid of; remove (9)
Guaranteed; for sure; certain (7)
Having calm endurance (7)
Having the ability (7)
Immeasurably great or large; boundless (8)
In the habit of; used to (10)
Intensity or sharpness (8)
Lacking respect and honor (11)
Not clearly; hazily; somewhat (7)
Of critical importance (5)
Parts; features; phases (7)
Persuade to adopt a particular belief (7)
Regional or social variety of a language (7)
Sets securely in place (8)
The act of intentionally killing oneself (7)
To endure; to put up with (8)
To express in words (9)
Unable to be avoided or escaped; certain (10)
Very great in area or extent; immense (4)
Wildly excited or enthusiastic (8)
Worthy of notice or attention (10)

Tears Of A Tiger Vocabulary Word Search 2 Answer Key

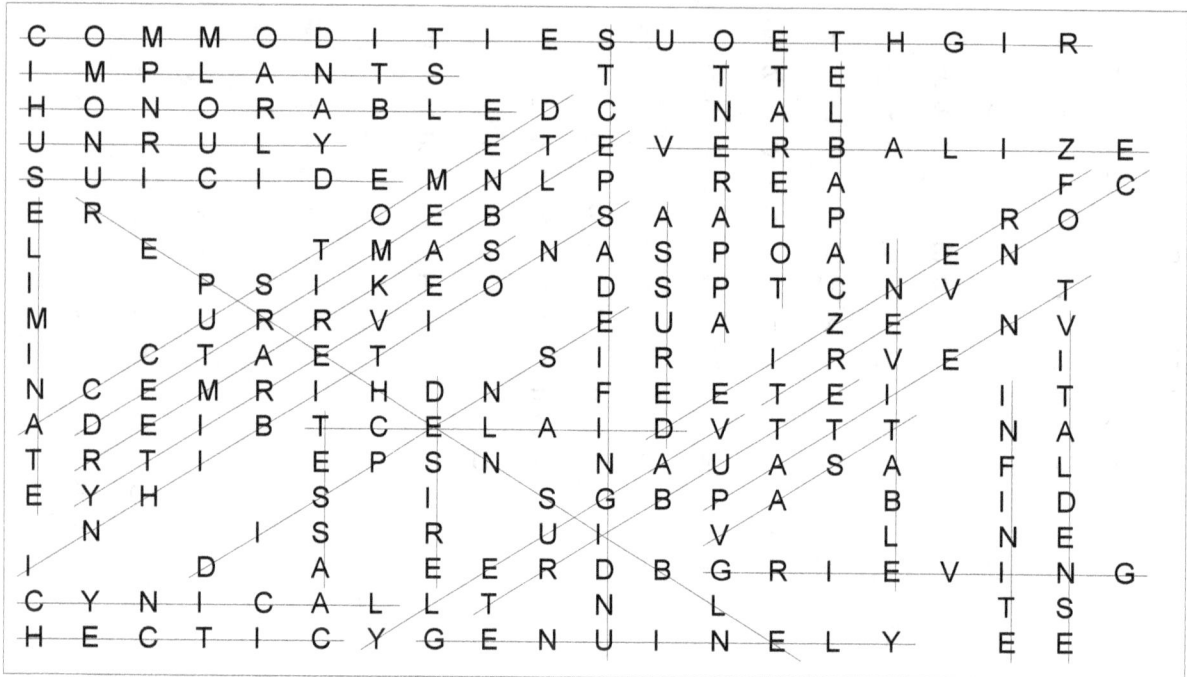

A cause of loss, damage, disadvantage, or injury (9)
A longing for; wanting (6)
A useful and desirable thing or quality (5)
Acting in an upright, moral way; virtuous (9)
Actually; really; authentically (9)
An acknowledgment of gratitude, respect, or admiration (7)
Articles of trade or commerce; products (11)
Characterized by intense activity, confusion, or haste (6)
Conscious or unconscious restraint of a behavior (11)
Deal out; distribute (8)
Deserving of reproof, rebuke, or censure; blameworthy (13)
Deserving or winning respect or distinction (9)
Difficult or impossible to discipline or control (6)
Difficult to understand or follow because of being closely packed with ideas or complex styles (5)
Distrusting or seeing the worst in the motives of others (7)

Easily perceived or understood (8)
Experiencing or expressing sorrow (8)
Get rid of; remove (9)
Guaranteed; for sure; certain (7)
Having calm endurance (7)
Having the ability (7)
Immeasurably great or large; boundless (8)
In the habit of; used to (10)
Intensity or sharpness (8)
Lacking respect and honor (11)
Not clearly; hazily; somewhat (7)
Of critical importance (5)
Parts; features; phases (7)
Persuade to adopt a particular belief (7)
Regional or social variety of a language (7)
Sets securely in place (8)
The act of intentionally killing oneself (7)
To endure; to put up with (8)
To express in words (9)
Unable to be avoided or escaped; certain (10)
Very great in area or extent; immense (4)
Wildly excited or enthusiastic (8)
Worthy of notice or attention (10)

Tears Of A Tiger Vocabulary Word Search 3

```
C D S E V E R I T Y S N O I T N E T N I
O D I A L E C T N D E I F I N G I D N U
N J C S S J F N S Y H I N F I N I T E T
V L J V P M R S X J E G H I M S R E L H
E B J D C E L U X J C C N M S U Q S I J
R H H J K A N B E N T C W S D O W S M Q
T E D I C I U S U O I L E B E R A I L
C Q N I W Z N T E D C C A C H T E U N D
A A N Z X E P A E R D O T N O H V N A X
C Y P V D H G N T A P N I A N G E R T Z
C C I A V X T T L B U F V B O I L U E X
U O M N B S V I M M N I T R R R A L F Q
S M P K E L B A W O I D R U A D T Y R T
T M L F N V E L S B T E I T B E I T E T
O O A V A L I T B V I N B S L S O O N B
M D N S G P C T L P V C U I E I N L Z C
E I T T N E I T A P E E T D T R W E I N
D T S H P H C Y N B D S E F S E C R E R
T I A S S U R E D Y L E U G A V Q A D Z
Z E A E L B A K R A M E R W N R V T T N
A S S I M I L A T E E Z I L A B R E V G
```

ACCUSTOMED	DENSE	INEVITABLE	SUBSTANTIAL
ASPECTS	DESIRE	INFINITE	SUICIDE
ASSET	DIALECT	INTENTIONS	TOLERATE
ASSIMILATE	DISPENSE	INTRUDE	TRIBUTE
ASSURED	DISTURBANCES	PATIENT	UNDIGNIFIED
BOMBARD	ELIMINATE	PUNITIVE	UNRULY
CAPABLE	FRENZIED	REBELLIOUS	VAGUELY
COMMODITIES	HECTIC	REMARKABLE	VAST
CONFIDENCES	HONORABLE	REVELATION	VERBALIZE
CONVERT	IMPLANTS	RIGHTEOUS	VITAL
CYNICAL	INCIDENTS	SEVERITY	

Tears Of A Tiger Vocabulary Word Search 3 Answer Key

ACCUSTOMED	DENSE	INEVITABLE	SUBSTANTIAL
ASPECTS	DESIRE	INFINITE	SUICIDE
ASSET	DIALECT	INTENTIONS	TOLERATE
ASSIMILATE	DISPENSE	INTRUDE	TRIBUTE
ASSURED	DISTURBANCES	PATIENT	UNDIGNIFIED
BOMBARD	ELIMINATE	PUNITIVE	UNRULY
CAPABLE	FRENZIED	REBELLIOUS	VAGUELY
COMMODITIES	HECTIC	REMARKABLE	VAST
CONFIDENCES	HONORABLE	REVELATION	VERBALIZE
CONVERT	IMPLANTS	RIGHTEOUS	VITAL
CYNICAL	INCIDENTS	SEVERITY	

Tears Of A Tiger Vocabulary Word Search 4

```
C O M M O D I T I E S R H E C T I C A H
O Y T E Q Z P N M T I E I C L N C M S V
N R N V D F C E P A N V H G W E O K P B
F E R I S E D M L N E O F H I N J E J
I D L T C S B I A U V N R A T V H C B
D I D I C A X R N T I A O E S A E V T D
E C I N M Z L T T R T R N S P R O S Z
N I S U H I H E S O A I A Z E D T V U X
C U T P E N N D P F B O B I T E S L V S
E S U G L C G A T Q L N L E W R C X L T
S V R R B I E H T Z E V E D W U Q G D L
B A B I I D N Z E E S N E D V S G E V C
P G A E S E U E L B A P C F S T V D F
V U N V N N I D B V Z Q S D R A B M O B
I E C I E T N T A P F T N E R A P P A B
T L E N H S E S K W Y L L E V R D G L J
A Y S G E Y L U R N U D P B V E L C V F
L G H D R L Y C A E T U B I R T R R A T
E S N E P S I D M G C E D U R T N I S Z
D I A L E C T P E E A S S I M I L A T E
T O L E R A T E R V E R B A L I Z E X Y
```

APPARENT	DENSE	HECTIC	REVELATION
ASPECTS	DESIRE	HONORABLE	RIGHTEOUS
ASSET	DETRIMENT	IMPLANTS	SEVERITY
ASSIMILATE	DIALECT	INCIDENTS	SUICIDE
ASSURED	DISPENSE	INEVITABLE	TOLERATE
BOMBARD	DISTURBANCES	INTRUDE	TRIBUTE
CAPABLE	ELIMINATE	PATIENT	UNRULY
COMMODITIES	FORTUNATE	PUNITIVE	VAGUELY
CONFIDENCES	FRENZIED	RECUPERATED	VAST
CONVERT	GENUINELY	REMARKABLE	VERBALIZE
CYNICAL	GRIEVING	REPREHENSIBLE	VITAL

Tears Of A Tiger Vocabulary Word Search 4 Answer Key

APPARENT	DENSE	HECTIC	REVELATION
ASPECTS	DESIRE	HONORABLE	RIGHTEOUS
ASSET	DETRIMENT	IMPLANTS	SEVERITY
ASSIMILATE	DIALECT	INCIDENTS	SUICIDE
ASSURED	DISPENSE	INEVITABLE	TOLERATE
BOMBARD	DISTURBANCES	INTRUDE	TRIBUTE
CAPABLE	ELIMINATE	PATIENT	UNRULY
COMMODITIES	FORTUNATE	PUNITIVE	VAGUELY
CONFIDENCES	FRENZIED	RECUPERATED	VAST
CONVERT	GENUINELY	REMARKABLE	VERBALIZE
CYNICAL	GRIEVING	REPREHENSIBLE	VITAL

Tears Of A Tiger Vocabulary Crossword 1

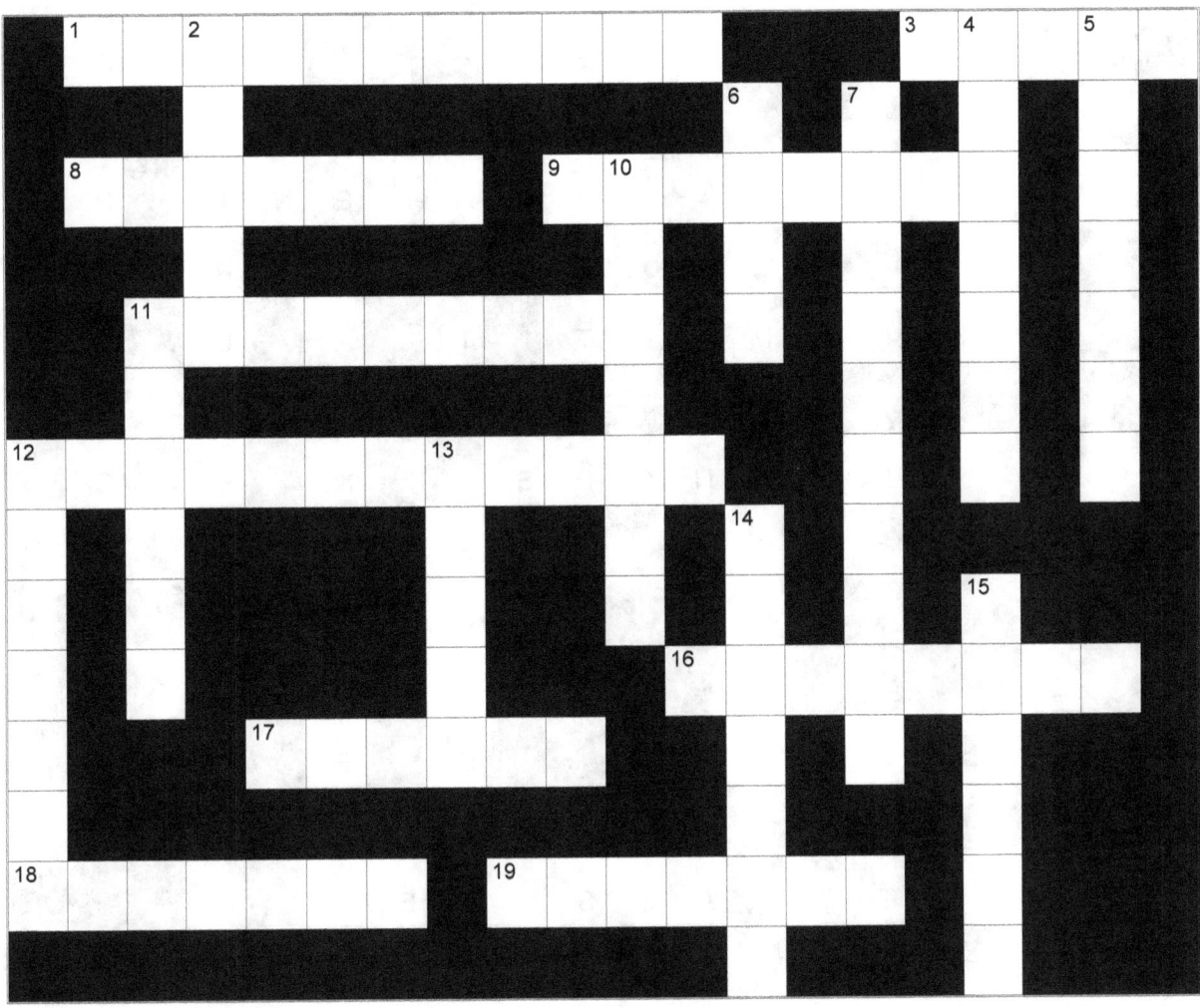

Across
1. Lacking respect and honor
3. Of critical importance
8. Distrusting or seeing the worst in the motives of others
9. Easily perceived or understood
11. A cause of loss, damage, disadvantage, or injury
12. Outbreaks of disorder; commotion
16. Sets securely in place
17. Characterized by intense activity, confusion, or haste
18. An acknowledgment of gratitude, respect, or admiration
19. Guaranteed; for sure; certain

Down
2. Difficult to understand or follow because of being closely packed with ideas or complex styles
4. Put or force in inappropriately, especially without permission
5. Parts; features; phases
6. Very great in area or extent; immense
7. Worthy of notice or attention
10. Having calm endurance
11. A longing for; wanting
12. Regional or social variety of a language
13. A useful and desirable thing or quality
14. To attack or assail, as with artillery or rapid fire
15. Difficult or impossible to discipline or control

Tears Of A Tiger Vocabulary Crossword 1 Answer Key

Across
1. Lacking respect and honor
3. Of critical importance
8. Distrusting or seeing the worst in the motives of others
9. Easily perceived or understood
11. A cause of loss, damage, disadvantage, or injury
12. Outbreaks of disorder; commotion
16. Sets securely in place
17. Characterized by intense activity, confusion, or haste
18. An acknowledgment of gratitude, respect, or admiration
19. Guaranteed; for sure; certain

Down
2. Difficult to understand or follow because of being closely packed with ideas or complex styles
4. Put or force in inappropriately, especially without permission
5. Parts; features; phases
6. Very great in area or extent; immense
7. Worthy of notice or attention
10. Having calm endurance
11. A longing for; wanting
12. Regional or social variety of a language
13. A useful and desirable thing or quality
14. To attack or assail, as with artillery or rapid fire
15. Difficult or impossible to discipline or control

Tears Of A Tiger Vocabulary Crossword 2

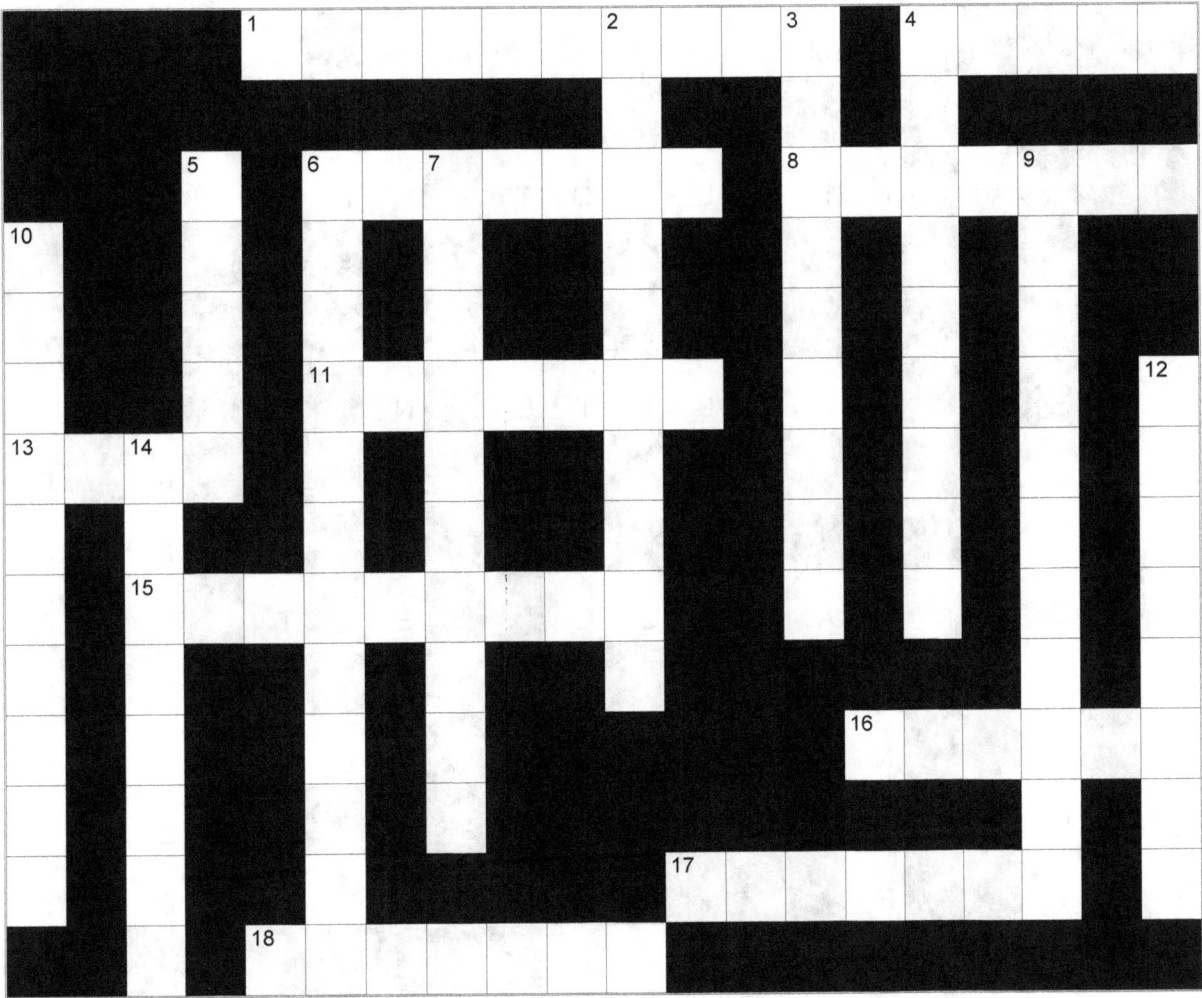

Across
1. Worthy of notice or attention
4. Difficult to understand or follow because of being closely packed with ideas or complex styles
6. Regional or social variety of a language
8. Put or force in inappropriately, especially without permission
11. An acknowledgment of gratitude, respect, or admiration
13. Very great in area or extent; immense
15. To express in words
16. A longing for; wanting
17. To attack or assail, as with artillery or rapid fire
18. Parts; features; phases

Down
2. In the habit of; used to
3. Get rid of; remove
4. A cause of loss, damage, disadvantage, or injury
5. A useful and desirable thing or quality
6. Outbreaks of disorder; commotion
7. Become a part of the main or dominant culture
9. Lacking respect and honor
10. Unable to be avoided or escaped; certain
12. Easily perceived or understood
14. Intensity or sharpness

Tears Of A Tiger Vocabulary Crossword 2 Answer Key

Across
1. Worthy of notice or attention
4. Difficult to understand or follow because of being closely packed with ideas or complex styles
6. Regional or social variety of a language
8. Put or force in inappropriately, especially without permission
11. An acknowledgment of gratitude, respect, or admiration
13. Very great in area or extent; immense
15. To express in words
16. A longing for; wanting
17. To attack or assail, as with artillery or rapid fire
18. Parts; features; phases

Down
2. In the habit of; used to
3. Get rid of; remove
4. A cause of loss, damage, disadvantage, or injury
5. A useful and desirable thing or quality
6. Outbreaks of disorder; commotion
7. Become a part of the main or dominant culture
9. Lacking respect and honor
10. Unable to be avoided or escaped; certain
12. Easily perceived or understood
14. Intensity or sharpness

1 Across: REMARKABLE
4 Across: DENSE
6 Across: DIALECT
8 Across: INTRUDE
11 Across: TRIBUTE
13 Across: VAST
15 Across: VERBALIZE
16 Across: DESIRE
17 Across: BOMBARD
18 Across: ASPECTS

2 Down: ACCUSTOMED
3 Down: ELIMINATE
4 Down: DETRIMENT
5 Down: ASSET
6 Down: DISTURBANCE
7 Down: ASSIMILATE
9 Down: UNDIGNIFIED
10 Down: INEVITABLE
12 Down: APPARENT
14 Down: SEVERITY

Tears Of A Tiger Vocabulary Crossword 3

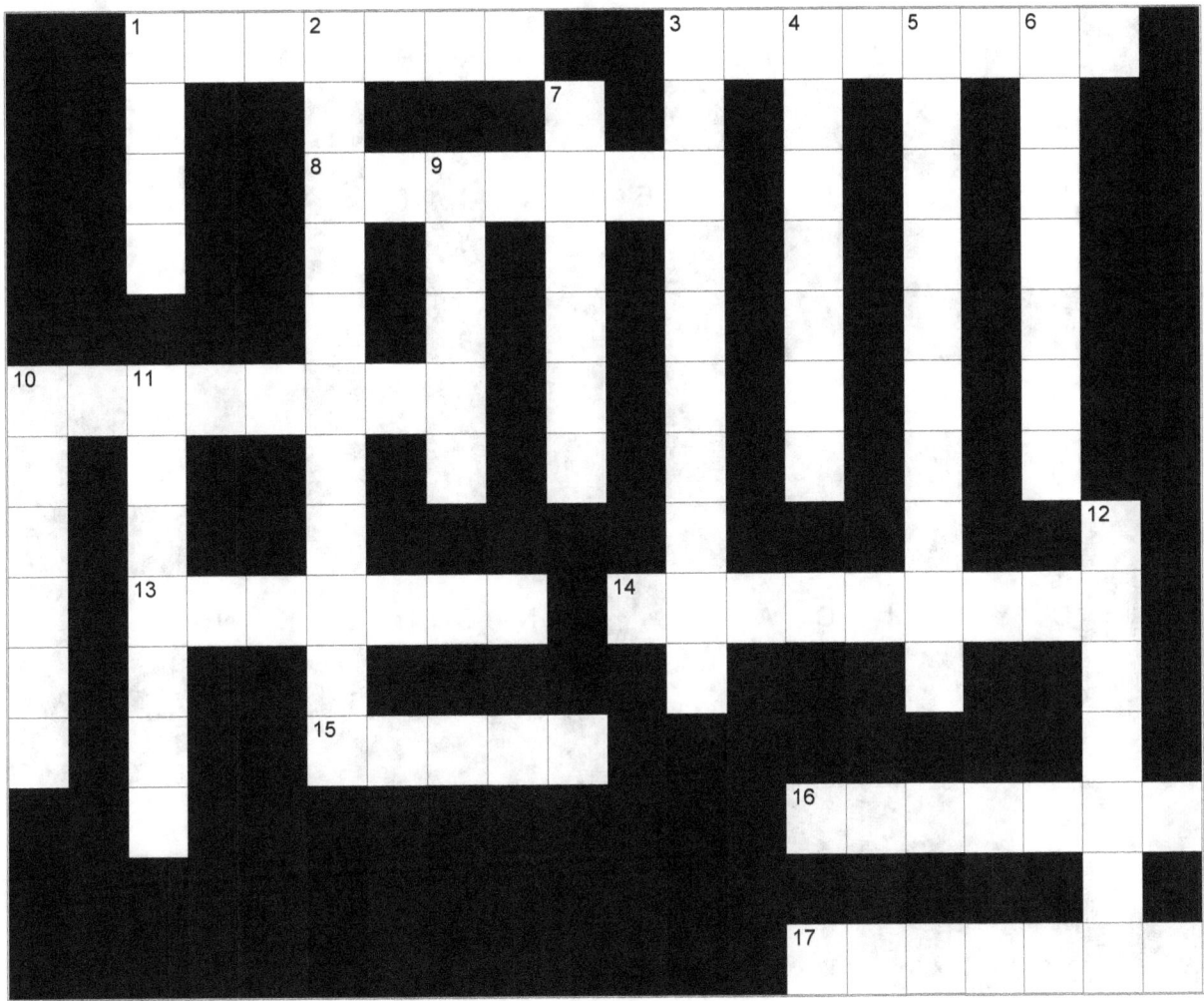

Across
1. Not clearly; hazily; somewhat
3. Sets securely in place
8. Regional or social variety of a language
10. Deal out; distribute
13. Distrusting or seeing the worst in the motives of others
14. Minor events
15. Difficult to understand or follow because of being closely packed with ideas or complex styles
16. To attack or assail, as with artillery or rapid fire
17. Put or force in inappropriately, especially without permission

Down
1. Very great in area or extent; immense
2. Lacking respect and honor
3. Objectives; motives
4. Having calm endurance
5. In the habit of; used to
6. An acknowledgment of gratitude, respect, or admiration
7. Characterized by intense activity, confusion, or haste
9. A useful and desirable thing or quality
10. A longing for; wanting
11. The act of intentionally killing oneself
12. Guaranteed; for sure; certain

Tears Of A Tiger Vocabulary Crossword 3 Answer Key

Across
1. Not clearly; hazily; somewhat
3. Sets securely in place
8. Regional or social variety of a language
10. Deal out; distribute
13. Distrusting or seeing the worst in the motives of others
14. Minor events
15. Difficult to understand or follow because of being closely packed with ideas or complex styles
16. To attack or assail, as with artillery or rapid fire
17. Put or force in inappropriately, especially without permission

Down
1. Very great in area or extent; immense
2. Lacking respect and honor
3. Objectives; motives
4. Having calm endurance
5. In the habit of; used to
6. An acknowledgment of gratitude, respect, or admiration
7. Characterized by intense activity, confusion, or haste
9. A useful and desirable thing or quality
10. A longing for; wanting
11. The act of intentionally killing oneself
12. Guaranteed; for sure; certain

Tears Of A Tiger Vocabulary Crossword 4

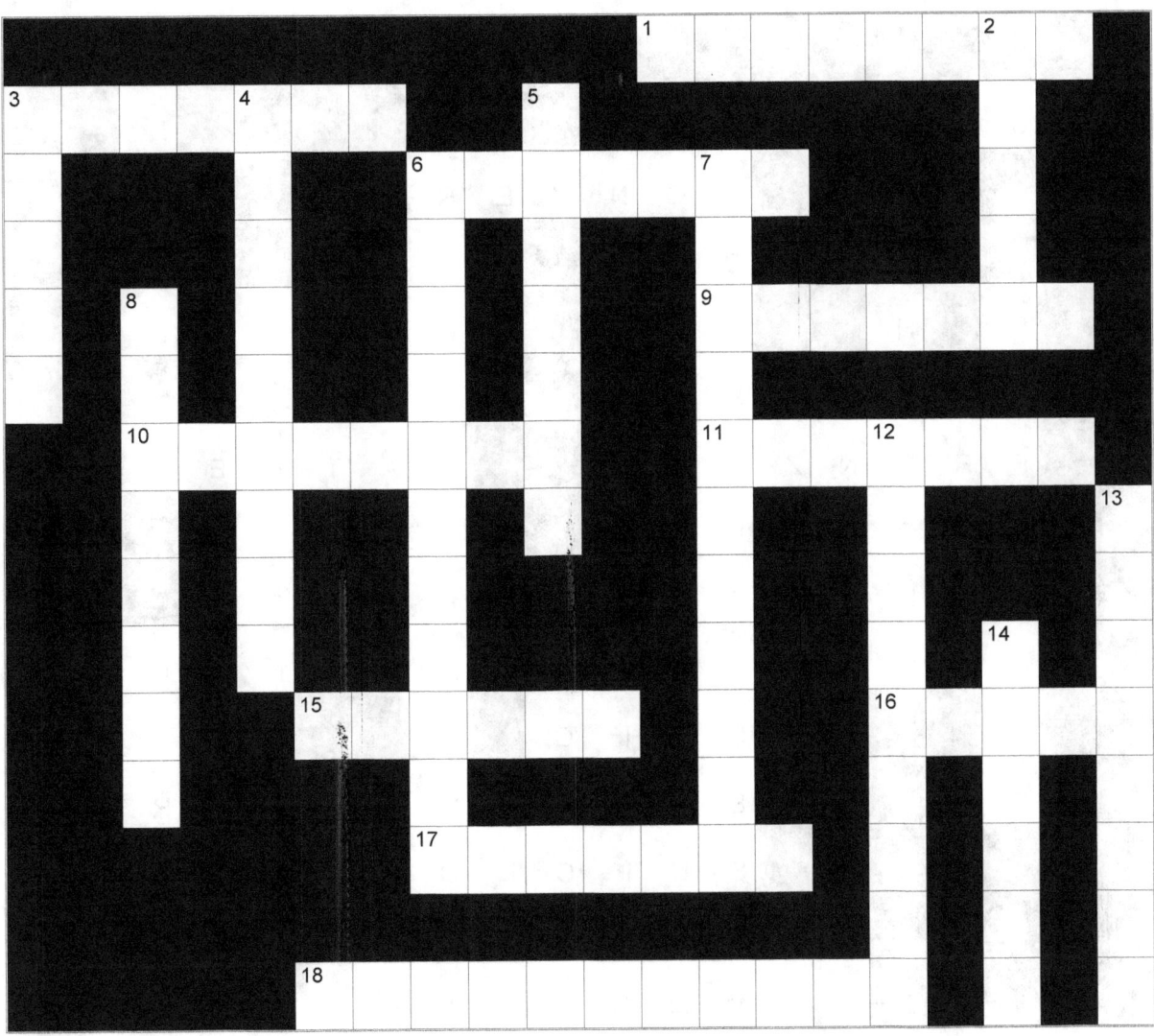

Across
1. Punishing
3. Guaranteed; for sure; certain
6. Persuade to adopt a particular belief
9. Having the ability
10. Wildly excited or enthusiastic
11. Having calm endurance
15. Characterized by intense activity, confusion, or haste
16. Difficult to understand or follow because of being closely packed with ideas or complex styles
17. The act of intentionally killing oneself
18. Articles of trade or commerce; products

Down
2. Of critical importance
3. A useful and desirable thing or quality
4. Acting in an upright, moral way; virtuous
5. Put or force in inappropriately, especially without permission
6. Feelings of assurance that a secret will be kept
7. Returned to health or strength; recovered
8. Immeasurably great or large; boundless
12. Minor events
13. To endure; to put up with
14. Difficult or impossible to discipline or control

Tears Of A Tiger Vocabulary Crossword 4 Answer Key

Across
1. Punishing
3. Guaranteed; for sure; certain
6. Persuade to adopt a particular belief
9. Having the ability
10. Wildly excited or enthusiastic
11. Having calm endurance
15. Characterized by intense activity, confusion, or haste
16. Difficult to understand or follow because of being closely packed with ideas or complex styles
17. The act of intentionally killing oneself
18. Articles of trade or commerce; products

Down
2. Of critical importance
3. A useful and desirable thing or quality
4. Acting in an upright, moral way; virtuous
5. Put or force in inappropriately, especially without permission
6. Feelings of assurance that a secret will be kept
7. Returned to health or strength; recovered
8. Immeasurably great or large; boundless
12. Minor events
13. To endure; to put up with
14. Difficult or impossible to discipline or control

Tears Of A Tiger Vocabulary Juggle Letters 1

1. FIIENTNI = 1. _____
   Immeasurably great or large; boundless

2. EMDCCTOAUS = 2. _____
   In the habit of; used to

3. NTESINDIC = 3. _____
   Minor events

4. INMIELETA = 4. _____
   Get rid of; remove

5. ESNDE = 5. _____
   Difficult to understand or follow because of being closely packed with ideas or complex styles

6. ISEREHBLNERPE = 6. _____
   Deserving of reproof, rebuke, or censure; blameworthy

7. ESAUDSR = 7. _____
   Guaranteed; for sure; certain

8. EDSEIR = 8. _____
   A longing for; wanting

9. EITRNLVEAO = 9. _____
   An enlightening or astonishing disclosure

10. RDOINIROTATEE =10. _____
    The process of growing worse, weakening, or declining

11. LSREULBIEO =11. _____
    Going against control or authority

12. LVEUAGY =12. _____
    Not clearly; hazily; somewhat

13. ACYLNIC =13. _____
    Distrusting or seeing the worst in the motives of others

14. ETNIPTA =14. _____
    Having calm endurance

Tears Of A Tiger Vocabulary Juggle Letters 1 Answer Key

1. FIIENTNI = 1. INFINITE
   Immeasurably great or large; boundless

2. EMDCCTOAUS = 2. ACCUSTOMED
   In the habit of; used to

3. NTESINDIC = 3. INCIDENTS
   Minor events

4. INMIELETA = 4. ELIMINATE
   Get rid of; remove

5. ESNDE = 5. DENSE
   Difficult to understand or follow because of being closely packed with ideas or complex styles

6. ISEREHBLNERPE = 6. REPREHENSIBLE
   Deserving of reproof, rebuke, or censure; blameworthy

7. ESAUDSR = 7. ASSURED
   Guaranteed; for sure; certain

8. EDSEIR = 8. DESIRE
   A longing for; wanting

9. EITRNLVEAO = 9. REVELATION
   An enlightening or astonishing disclosure

10. RDOINIROTATEE = 10. DETERIORATION
    The process of growing worse, weakening, or declining

11. LSREULBIEO = 11. REBELLIOUS
    Going against control or authority

12. LVEUAGY = 12. VAGUELY
    Not clearly; hazily; somewhat

13. ACYLNIC = 13. CYNICAL
    Distrusting or seeing the worst in the motives of others

14. ETNIPTA = 14. PATIENT
    Having calm endurance

Tears Of A Tiger Vocabulary Juggle Letters 2

1. ALNMETEII = 1. _____
Get rid of; remove

2. ASSICNTRDEBU = 2. _____
Outbreaks of disorder; commotion

3. USHTGRIOE = 3. _____
Acting in an upright, moral way; virtuous

4. ILTVA = 4. _____
Of critical importance

5. EVIANBLIET = 5. _____
Unable to be avoided or escaped; certain

6. AEVULGY = 6. _____
Not clearly; hazily; somewhat

7. ERCNTOV = 7. _____
Persuade to adopt a particular belief

8. EBEPSILERHERN = 8. _____
Deserving of reproof, rebuke, or censure; blameworthy

9. NINNIEOTST = 9. _____
Objectives; motives

10. PRNPAAET = 10. _____
Easily perceived or understood

11. ASNTLUIBSAT = 11. _____
Of ample or considerable amount

12. ENESD = 12. _____
Difficult to understand or follow because of being closely packed with ideas or complex styles

13. INEZFRDE = 13. _____
Wildly excited or enthusiastic

14. ESEINPSD = 14. _____
Deal out; distribute

Tears Of A Tiger Vocabulary Juggle Letters 2 Answer Key

1. ALNMETEII = 1. ELIMINATE
   Get rid of; remove

2. ASSICNTRDEBU = 2. DISTURBANCES
   Outbreaks of disorder; commotion

3. USHTGRIOE = 3. RIGHTEOUS
   Acting in an upright, moral way; virtuous

4. ILTVA = 4. VITAL
   Of critical importance

5. EVIANBLIET = 5. INEVITABLE
   Unable to be avoided or escaped; certain

6. AEVULGY = 6. VAGUELY
   Not clearly; hazily; somewhat

7. ERCNTOV = 7. CONVERT
   Persuade to adopt a particular belief

8. EBEPSILERHERN = 8. REPREHENSIBLE
   Deserving of reproof, rebuke, or censure; blameworthy

9. NINNIEOTST = 9. INTENTIONS
   Objectives; motives

10. PRNPAAET = 10. APPARENT
    Easily perceived or understood

11. ASNTLUIBSAT = 11. SUBSTANTIAL
    Of ample or considerable amount

12. ENESD = 12. DENSE
    Difficult to understand or follow because of being closely packed with ideas or complex styles

13. INEZFRDE = 13. FRENZIED
    Wildly excited or enthusiastic

14. ESEINPSD = 14. DISPENSE
    Deal out; distribute

Tears Of A Tiger Vocabulary Juggle Letters 3

1. SBOEEULLIR = 1. _____
   Going against control or authority

2. CIETLDA = 2. _____
   Regional or social variety of a language

3. NALETIMEI = 3. _____
   Get rid of; remove

4. ENUIDFINDIG = 4. _____
   Lacking respect and honor

5. TPPERAAN = 5. _____
   Easily perceived or understood

6. ISSENEPD = 6. _____
   Deal out; distribute

7. INIBSHIONTI = 7. _____
   Conscious or unconscious restraint of a behavior

8. NTIURED = 8. _____
   Put or force in inappropriately, especially without permission

9. NINTIEDSC = 9. _____
   Minor events

10. TESSA = 10. _____
    A useful and desirable thing or quality

11. TAEPSSC = 11. _____
    Parts; features; phases

12. ETASLIMAIS = 12. _____
    Become a part of the main or dominant culture

13. VAZBRLEEI = 13. _____
    To express in words

14. ODTSIMOMIEC = 14. _____
    Articles of trade or commerce; products

Tears Of A Tiger Vocabulary Juggle Letters 3 Answer Key

1. SBOEEULLIR = 1. REBELLIOUS
   Going against control or authority

2. CIETLDA = 2. DIALECT
   Regional or social variety of a language

3. NALETIMEI = 3. ELIMINATE
   Get rid of; remove

4. ENUIDFINDIG = 4. UNDIGNIFIED
   Lacking respect and honor

5. TPPERAAN = 5. APPARENT
   Easily perceived or understood

6. ISSENEPD = 6. DISPENSE
   Deal out; distribute

7. INIBSHIONTI = 7. INHIBITIONS
   Conscious or unconscious restraint of a behavior

8. NTIURED = 8. INTRUDE
   Put or force in inappropriately, especially without permission

9. NINTIEDSC = 9. INCIDENTS
   Minor events

10. TESSA = 10. ASSET
    A useful and desirable thing or quality

11. TAEPSSC = 11. ASPECTS
    Parts; features; phases

12. ETASLIMAIS = 12. ASSIMILATE
    Become a part of the main or dominant culture

13. VAZBRLEEI = 13. VERBALIZE
    To express in words

14. ODTSIMOMIEC = 14. COMMODITIES
    Articles of trade or commerce; products

Tears Of A Tiger Vocabulary Juggle Letters 4

1. ALREBVIZE = 1. _____
To express in words

2. LCYNICA = 2. _____
Distrusting or seeing the worst in the motives of others

3. LRSEIEBOUL = 3. _____
Going against control or authority

4. ERVGNIGI = 4. _____
Experiencing or expressing sorrow

5. MTEEINTDR = 5. _____
A cause of loss, damage, disadvantage, or injury

6. NTNSEIINOT = 6. _____
Objectives; motives

7. SADUSER = 7. _____
Guaranteed; for sure; certain

8. ILCADTE = 8. _____
Regional or social variety of a language

9. NDSEPEIS = 9. _____
Deal out; distribute

10. EEIDRS = 10. _____
A longing for; wanting

11. IBRETUT = 11. _____
An acknowledgment of gratitude, respect, or admiration

12. INNFEIDDIGU = 12. _____
Lacking respect and honor

13. EOOIRATRITNED = 13. _____
The process of growing worse, weakening, or declining

14. GRHISOUTE = 14. _____
Acting in an upright, moral way; virtuous

Tears Of A Tiger Vocabulary Juggle Letters 4 Answer Key

1. ALREBVIZE = 1. VERBALIZE
To express in words

2. LCYNICA = 2. CYNICAL
Distrusting or seeing the worst in the motives of others

3. LRSEIEBOUL = 3. REBELLIOUS
Going against control or authority

4. ERVGNIGI = 4. GRIEVING
Experiencing or expressing sorrow

5. MTEEINTDR = 5. DETRIMENT
A cause of loss, damage, disadvantage, or injury

6. NTNSEIINOT = 6. INTENTIONS
Objectives; motives

7. SADUSER = 7. ASSURED
Guaranteed; for sure; certain

8. ILCADTE = 8. DIALECT
Regional or social variety of a language

9. NDSEPEIS = 9. DISPENSE
Deal out; distribute

10. EEIDRS = 10. DESIRE
A longing for; wanting

11. IBRETUT = 11. TRIBUTE
An acknowledgment of gratitude, respect, or admiration

12. INNFEIDDIGU = 12. UNDIGNIFIED
Lacking respect and honor

13. EOOIRATRITNED = 13. DETERIORATION
The process of growing worse, weakening, or declining

14. GRHISOUTE = 14. RIGHTEOUS
Acting in an upright, moral way; virtuous

ACCUSTOMED	In the habit of; used to
APPARENT	Easily perceived or understood
ASPECTS	Parts; features; phases
ASSET	A useful and desirable thing or quality
ASSIMILATE	Become a part of the main or dominant culture
ASSURED	Guaranteed; for sure; certain

BOMBARD	To attack or assail, as with artillery or rapid fire
CAPABLE	Having the ability
COMMODITIES	Articles of trade or commerce; products
CONFIDENCES	Feelings of assurance that a secret will be kept
CONVERT	Persuade to adopt a particular belief
CYNICAL	Distrusting or seeing the worst in the motives of others

DENSE	Difficult to understand or follow because of being closely packed with ideas or complex styles
DESIRE	A longing for; wanting
DETERIORATION	The process of growing worse, weakening, or declining
DETRIMENT	A cause of loss, damage, disadvantage, or injury
DIALECT	Regional or social variety of a language
DISPENSE	Deal out; distribute

DISTURBANCES	Outbreaks of disorder; commotion
ELIMINATE	Get rid of; remove
FORTUNATE	Lucky
FRENZIED	Wildly excited or enthusiastic
GENUINELY	Actually; really; authentically
GRIEVING	Experiencing or expressing sorrow

HECTIC	Characterized by intense activity, confusion, or haste
HONORABLE	Deserving or winning respect or distinction
IMPLANTS	Sets securely in place
INCIDENTS	Minor events
INEVITABLE	Unable to be avoided or escaped; certain
INFINITE	Immeasurably great or large; boundless

INHIBITIONS	Conscious or unconscious restraint of a behavior
INTENTIONS	Objectives; motives
INTRUDE	Put or force in inappropriately, especially without permission
PATIENT	Having calm endurance
PUNITIVE	Punishing
REBELLIOUS	Going against control or authority

RECUPERATED	Returned to health or strength; recovered
REMARKABLE	Worthy of notice or attention
REPREHENSIBLE	Deserving of reproof, rebuke, or censure; blameworthy
REVELATION	An enlightening or astonishing disclosure
RIGHTEOUS	Acting in an upright, moral way; virtuous
SEVERITY	Intensity or sharpness

SUBSTANTIAL	Of ample or considerable amount
SUICIDE	The act of intentionally killing oneself
TOLERATE	To endure; to put up with
TRIBUTE	An acknowledgment of gratitude, respect, or admiration
UNDIGNIFIED	Lacking respect and honor
UNRULY	Difficult or impossible to discipline or control

VAGUELY	Not clearly; hazily; somewhat
VAST	Very great in area or extent; immense
VERBALIZE	To express in words
VITAL	Of critical importance

Tears Of A Tiger Vocabulary

ASSURED	RECUPERATED	HECTIC	REMARKABLE	CONVERT
APPARENT	INTENTIONS	TRIBUTE	ASPECTS	CONFIDENCES
INFINITE	SUICIDE	FREE SPACE	VAGUELY	DETERIORATION
ELIMINATE	DENSE	VAST	REVELATION	PUNITIVE
INHIBITIONS	INTRUDE	GRIEVING	DIALECT	SEVERITY

Tears Of A Tiger Vocabulary

DISPENSE	HONORABLE	ACCUSTOMED	CYNICAL	UNDIGNIFIED
REPREHENSIBLE	SUBSTANTIAL	FRENZIED	VITAL	DESIRE
ASSIMILATE	IMPLANTS	FREE SPACE	INEVITABLE	ASSET
TOLERATE	RIGHTEOUS	FORTUNATE	DISTURBANCES	PATIENT
UNRULY	REBELLIOUS	COMMODITIES	INCIDENTS	VERBALIZE

Tears Of A Tiger Vocabulary

DISPENSE	UNRULY	ACCUSTOMED	INFINITE	APPARENT
RECUPERATED	VAGUELY	INCIDENTS	VITAL	FORTUNATE
ASSIMILATE	FRENZIED	FREE SPACE	HECTIC	ELIMINATE
RIGHTEOUS	REPREHENSIBLE	PATIENT	INEVITABLE	REVELATION
DESIRE	CONFIDENCES	VERBALIZE	SEVERITY	CAPABLE

Tears Of A Tiger Vocabulary

ASSURED	REMARKABLE	TRIBUTE	DIALECT	REBELLIOUS
COMMODITIES	BOMBARD	ASPECTS	IMPLANTS	DETRIMENT
INTRUDE	SUBSTANTIAL	FREE SPACE	INHIBITIONS	DETERIORATION
CONVERT	HONORABLE	GRIEVING	UNDIGNIFIED	TOLERATE
GENUINELY	VAST	SUICIDE	INTENTIONS	PUNITIVE

Tears Of A Tiger Vocabulary

FRENZIED	INFINITE	COMMODITIES	TOLERATE	SUBSTANTIAL
DISTURBANCES	CAPABLE	VERBALIZE	SUICIDE	PATIENT
ASSIMILATE	REBELLIOUS	FREE SPACE	REMARKABLE	PUNITIVE
INCIDENTS	SEVERITY	ASSET	BOMBARD	INEVITABLE
GRIEVING	CONFIDENCES	RECUPERATED	ASPECTS	HONORABLE

Tears Of A Tiger Vocabulary

CYNICAL	VITAL	CONVERT	DETERIORATION	DISPENSE
ASSURED	DIALECT	HECTIC	INTRUDE	RIGHTEOUS
INTENTIONS	DESIRE	FREE SPACE	DENSE	INHIBITIONS
APPARENT	GENUINELY	IMPLANTS	REVELATION	REPREHENSIBLE
DETRIMENT	ELIMINATE	FORTUNATE	VAST	UNRULY

Tears Of A Tiger Vocabulary

CYNICAL	CAPABLE	DENSE	APPARENT	ELIMINATE
SEVERITY	REBELLIOUS	GENUINELY	UNRULY	ASPECTS
FRENZIED	ASSIMILATE	FREE SPACE	DIALECT	REVELATION
INTRUDE	CONVERT	INEVITABLE	HONORABLE	ASSURED
TOLERATE	UNDIGNIFIED	VITAL	HECTIC	DETERIORATION

Tears Of A Tiger Vocabulary

RECUPERATED	INCIDENTS	CONFIDENCES	REMARKABLE	DISPENSE
INFINITE	DISTURBANCES	DESIRE	SUBSTANTIAL	INHIBITIONS
TRIBUTE	ASSET	FREE SPACE	REPREHENSIBLE	SUICIDE
INTENTIONS	PATIENT	RIGHTEOUS	IMPLANTS	COMMODITIES
DETRIMENT	VAST	GRIEVING	FORTUNATE	BOMBARD

Tears Of A Tiger Vocabulary

UNDIGNIFIED	FRENZIED	INTENTIONS	INFINITE	VERBALIZE
CYNICAL	CONFIDENCES	HONORABLE	VAST	REMARKABLE
DENSE	REPREHENSIBLE	FREE SPACE	HECTIC	DETRIMENT
ASPECTS	DETERIORATION	ASSURED	TOLERATE	DISTURBANCES
REBELLIOUS	ASSIMILATE	INCIDENTS	VITAL	APPARENT

Tears Of A Tiger Vocabulary

RECUPERATED	INTRUDE	INEVITABLE	CAPABLE	SUBSTANTIAL
RIGHTEOUS	PUNITIVE	CONVERT	DISPENSE	ELIMINATE
PATIENT	ACCUSTOMED	FREE SPACE	COMMODITIES	ASSET
FORTUNATE	REVELATION	SUICIDE	TRIBUTE	SEVERITY
GENUINELY	DIALECT	DESIRE	VAGUELY	BOMBARD

Tears Of A Tiger Vocabulary

COMMODITIES	REPREHENSIBLE	VAST	ASSIMILATE	ACCUSTOMED
SUBSTANTIAL	RECUPERATED	ASPECTS	DETRIMENT	HONORABLE
INEVITABLE	INFINITE	FREE SPACE	DISTURBANCES	INHIBITIONS
CONFIDENCES	ASSURED	DISPENSE	INCIDENTS	REVELATION
APPARENT	REMARKABLE	VERBALIZE	CAPABLE	UNDIGNIFIED

Tears Of A Tiger Vocabulary

IMPLANTS	RIGHTEOUS	ASSET	GRIEVING	VAGUELY
DIALECT	ELIMINATE	PUNITIVE	SUICIDE	TRIBUTE
BOMBARD	FORTUNATE	FREE SPACE	DENSE	HECTIC
GENUINELY	CONVERT	INTENTIONS	UNRULY	INTRUDE
DETERIORATION	TOLERATE	REBELLIOUS	CYNICAL	DESIRE

Tears Of A Tiger Vocabulary

CYNICAL	DENSE	INTRUDE	DIALECT	GRIEVING
SEVERITY	FRENZIED	ACCUSTOMED	ELIMINATE	RIGHTEOUS
IMPLANTS	PUNITIVE	FREE SPACE	RECUPERATED	ASSIMILATE
SUICIDE	INCIDENTS	INHIBITIONS	APPARENT	REVELATION
UNRULY	CONFIDENCES	REBELLIOUS	INEVITABLE	VAGUELY

Tears Of A Tiger Vocabulary

SUBSTANTIAL	TRIBUTE	VITAL	CONVERT	ASPECTS
REPREHENSIBLE	BOMBARD	DISPENSE	GENUINELY	DETERIORATION
COMMODITIES	ASSET	FREE SPACE	DISTURBANCES	DETRIMENT
PATIENT	INTENTIONS	INFINITE	FORTUNATE	UNDIGNIFIED
DESIRE	ASSURED	VERBALIZE	CAPABLE	REMARKABLE

Tears Of A Tiger Vocabulary

INFINITE	IMPLANTS	DETERIORATION	VAST	ASPECTS
ELIMINATE	HECTIC	TOLERATE	VAGUELY	ACCUSTOMED
CAPABLE	FORTUNATE	FREE SPACE	REPREHENSIBLE	ASSIMILATE
ASSET	VITAL	TRIBUTE	BOMBARD	REBELLIOUS
VERBALIZE	SEVERITY	PUNITIVE	FRENZIED	DETRIMENT

Tears Of A Tiger Vocabulary

INTENTIONS	PATIENT	UNDIGNIFIED	CONVERT	CONFIDENCES
HONORABLE	DESIRE	UNRULY	SUICIDE	COMMODITIES
INEVITABLE	CYNICAL	FREE SPACE	INTRUDE	APPARENT
DISPENSE	RIGHTEOUS	INHIBITIONS	REVELATION	GRIEVING
GENUINELY	DIALECT	REMARKABLE	ASSURED	SUBSTANTIAL

Tears Of A Tiger Vocabulary

GENUINELY	ELIMINATE	HONORABLE	INTRUDE	REMARKABLE
DISPENSE	INTENTIONS	TOLERATE	RIGHTEOUS	APPARENT
ACCUSTOMED	IMPLANTS	FREE SPACE	CONVERT	REPREHENSIBLE
SUBSTANTIAL	SEVERITY	CONFIDENCES	PUNITIVE	VAST
HECTIC	DESIRE	DETRIMENT	SUICIDE	ASPECTS

Tears Of A Tiger Vocabulary

REVELATION	INHIBITIONS	ASSURED	RECUPERATED	REBELLIOUS
CYNICAL	GRIEVING	INCIDENTS	FRENZIED	ASSET
COMMODITIES	DIALECT	FREE SPACE	DETERIORATION	VAGUELY
DISTURBANCES	DENSE	UNDIGNIFIED	VITAL	FORTUNATE
VERBALIZE	PATIENT	CAPABLE	BOMBARD	ASSIMILATE

Tears Of A Tiger Vocabulary

GENUINELY	CYNICAL	PATIENT	VAST	REPREHENSIBLE
REMARKABLE	INCIDENTS	VAGUELY	FRENZIED	BOMBARD
UNDIGNIFIED	DETRIMENT	FREE SPACE	ASSET	INTENTIONS
DISTURBANCES	INHIBITIONS	HECTIC	PUNITIVE	HONORABLE
ASSIMILATE	VERBALIZE	CONFIDENCES	VITAL	INTRUDE

Tears Of A Tiger Vocabulary

RIGHTEOUS	REVELATION	APPARENT	RECUPERATED	DESIRE
SUICIDE	DISPENSE	COMMODITIES	INFINITE	INEVITABLE
CAPABLE	ACCUSTOMED	FREE SPACE	IMPLANTS	GRIEVING
UNRULY	SEVERITY	SUBSTANTIAL	DIALECT	TRIBUTE
DETERIORATION	REBELLIOUS	TOLERATE	CONVERT	ASSURED

Tears Of A Tiger Vocabulary

ASSET	BOMBARD	REVELATION	DISTURBANCES	RIGHTEOUS
IMPLANTS	UNDIGNIFIED	CONVERT	ASSURED	SUICIDE
DESIRE	CYNICAL	FREE SPACE	INTRUDE	ACCUSTOMED
REBELLIOUS	DIALECT	FORTUNATE	DETERIORATION	REPREHENSIBLE
INCIDENTS	GENUINELY	TOLERATE	RECUPERATED	DETRIMENT

Tears Of A Tiger Vocabulary

VAST	INFINITE	INEVITABLE	ELIMINATE	UNRULY
ASSIMILATE	HONORABLE	INHIBITIONS	GRIEVING	REMARKABLE
VAGUELY	SEVERITY	FREE SPACE	FRENZIED	SUBSTANTIAL
VITAL	PUNITIVE	COMMODITIES	PATIENT	DENSE
CAPABLE	VERBALIZE	APPARENT	INTENTIONS	HECTIC

Tears Of A Tiger Vocabulary

INTRUDE	INTENTIONS	DISPENSE	GENUINELY	INEVITABLE
CAPABLE	ACCUSTOMED	UNRULY	SEVERITY	REMARKABLE
REBELLIOUS	TRIBUTE	FREE SPACE	INCIDENTS	VAGUELY
ELIMINATE	PUNITIVE	RIGHTEOUS	CONFIDENCES	VAST
HECTIC	CONVERT	COMMODITIES	INHIBITIONS	DENSE

Tears Of A Tiger Vocabulary

DESIRE	ASSURED	ASSET	HONORABLE	GRIEVING
CYNICAL	VITAL	IMPLANTS	DIALECT	SUICIDE
REPREHENSIBLE	BOMBARD	FREE SPACE	PATIENT	FRENZIED
SUBSTANTIAL	DETERIORATION	ASPECTS	TOLERATE	RECUPERATED
ASSIMILATE	DETRIMENT	DISTURBANCES	FORTUNATE	UNDIGNIFIED

Tears Of A Tiger Vocabulary

GRIEVING	RIGHTEOUS	HONORABLE	UNRULY	INTRUDE
ELIMINATE	APPARENT	ASSET	ACCUSTOMED	TRIBUTE
REPREHENSIBLE	GENUINELY	FREE SPACE	INFINITE	FORTUNATE
DETRIMENT	RECUPERATED	HECTIC	IMPLANTS	COMMODITIES
UNDIGNIFIED	ASPECTS	DISTURBANCES	SEVERITY	CONFIDENCES

Tears Of A Tiger Vocabulary

ASSIMILATE	ASSURED	BOMBARD	PATIENT	DESIRE
CONVERT	VITAL	INHIBITIONS	INEVITABLE	TOLERATE
INCIDENTS	CAPABLE	FREE SPACE	INTENTIONS	DISPENSE
REMARKABLE	SUBSTANTIAL	VERBALIZE	CYNICAL	PUNITIVE
FRENZIED	SUICIDE	DETERIORATION	DENSE	VAGUELY

Tears Of A Tiger Vocabulary

ASPECTS	UNDIGNIFIED	ASSURED	DISPENSE	DETERIORATION
VAST	HECTIC	REBELLIOUS	GRIEVING	VITAL
VAGUELY	REVELATION	FREE SPACE	BOMBARD	DIALECT
UNRULY	REMARKABLE	FRENZIED	DESIRE	DETRIMENT
INTRUDE	RIGHTEOUS	TRIBUTE	SEVERITY	SUBSTANTIAL

Tears Of A Tiger Vocabulary

RECUPERATED	HONORABLE	ASSIMILATE	TOLERATE	COMMODITIES
IMPLANTS	INCIDENTS	ASSET	DENSE	INFINITE
CONFIDENCES	INEVITABLE	FREE SPACE	ELIMINATE	REPREHENSIBLE
GENUINELY	INHIBITIONS	CYNICAL	PATIENT	PUNITIVE
DISTURBANCES	ACCUSTOMED	APPARENT	INTENTIONS	VERBALIZE

Tears Of A Tiger Vocabulary

FORTUNATE	INTRUDE	HECTIC	SUBSTANTIAL	ASSIMILATE
REPREHENSIBLE	REBELLIOUS	BOMBARD	RECUPERATED	ACCUSTOMED
RIGHTEOUS	FRENZIED	FREE SPACE	GRIEVING	ASSURED
CONVERT	CAPABLE	IMPLANTS	GENUINELY	DISPENSE
VAST	CYNICAL	INFINITE	VERBALIZE	DETRIMENT

Tears Of A Tiger Vocabulary

COMMODITIES	DETERIORATION	SEVERITY	ELIMINATE	VAGUELY
REMARKABLE	DESIRE	INEVITABLE	REVELATION	ASSET
APPARENT	DISTURBANCES	FREE SPACE	SUICIDE	UNDIGNIFIED
DIALECT	TRIBUTE	PATIENT	VITAL	CONFIDENCES
UNRULY	TOLERATE	INCIDENTS	HONORABLE	INTENTIONS

Tears Of A Tiger Vocabulary

ASSIMILATE	DENSE	REMARKABLE	SUBSTANTIAL	PATIENT
COMMODITIES	INCIDENTS	VITAL	ELIMINATE	FORTUNATE
VAST	ASPECTS	FREE SPACE	REBELLIOUS	GRIEVING
CONFIDENCES	UNRULY	CONVERT	IMPLANTS	UNDIGNIFIED
DISPENSE	HECTIC	DETRIMENT	ASSURED	RIGHTEOUS

Tears Of A Tiger Vocabulary

CAPABLE	DETERIORATION	SUICIDE	INTENTIONS	DISTURBANCES
CYNICAL	SEVERITY	BOMBARD	HONORABLE	ACCUSTOMED
INEVITABLE	DIALECT	FREE SPACE	GENUINELY	TOLERATE
VAGUELY	RECUPERATED	REVELATION	REPREHENSIBLE	INHIBITIONS
INFINITE	TRIBUTE	VERBALIZE	FRENZIED	APPARENT

www.ingramcontent.com/pod-product-compliance
Lightning Source LLC
Chambersburg PA
CBHW081456070526
44586CB00019B/2376